THE NATIONAL TRUST GARDENS HANDBOOK

NEW EDITION

THE NATIONAL TRUST

36 Queen Anne's Gate · London SW1H 9AS

Registered Charity No. 205846

Editor: ALISON HONEY
Illustrations by: ELIZABETH JANE LLOYD

Front cover: Octavia Hill Rose.
Photo: Stephen Dalton.
Back cover: The Vegetable Garden at Alfriston Clergy House.
Photo: National Trust Photographic Library/Andrew Butler.

ISBN 0 7078 0200 8

First published in Great Britain in 1991
Reprinted 1992
New edition 1993; reprinted 1993
New edition 1995; reprinted 1996
by National Trust Enterprises Limited,
36 Queen Anne's Gate, London SW1H 9AS

Designed by Pardoe Blacker Ltd, Lingfield, Surrey
Phototypeset in Monotype Bembo, Series 270
by Southern Positives and Negatives (SPAN), Lingfield, Surrey (9730)
Printed by Clays Ltd, Bungay, Suffolk

Contents

Introduction *page* 5

How to use this Handbook 9

THE GARDENS 11

South-West England 13

Southern England 33

Wales and the Welsh Borders 57

London, Thames Valley and the Chilterns 76

Heart of England 85

Eastern Counties 105

North-West England 115

North-East England 120

Northern Ireland 129

Maps 135

INFORMATION 143

Regional Offices 144

Useful Addresses 145

A Calendar for Visiting 147

National Trust Gardens by Category 153

Gardens & parks with early formal features 153

Gardens & parks with pre-Victorian landscape features 154

Gardens with Victorian & Edwardian features 155
Inter-war gardens 156
Post-war gardens 157
Rose gardens & rose beds 157
Herb gardens & borders 158
Fruit & vegetables 159
Rare trees & shrubs 160
Water gardens & waterside planting 161
Herbaceous & mixed borders 162
Topiary 163
Rock gardens 164
Conservatories 164
Orangeries 164
Grottoes 165
Gardens registered in the *Woody Plant Catalogue* 165
NCCPG National Collections in National Trust gardens 166

New Gardens 168

National Trust Gardening Books 171

National Trust for Scotland Gardens 173

Index of Gardens 174

Introduction

WHEN WE BEGAN TO COMPILE this Handbook, we found ourselves asking the most basic questions. There is no doubt that the National Trust has many gardens in its care – probably the largest collection in the world – but what constitutes a garden? How many can the National Trust claim to look after? How many should this book describe? After much discussion, we came to the conclusion that the National Trust looks after about 126 gardens which merit inclusion. These are either gardens in their own right, or gardens attached to a house but which are of interest and importance to a garden lover. Sometimes a garden opens out into a park, as at Calke Abbey in Derbyshire. Designing parks is a large-scale form of gardening but, for the purposes of this book, parks without gardens are not included, nor are landscaped pieces of scenery, like Tarn Hows in the Lake District, nor are gardens that are merely an adjunct to a house, like Lower Brockhampton in Hereford & Worcester.

This does not mean that we have short-changed you: within the gardens detailed here, there is a huge variety of types and sizes, from the landscaped masterpieces of Stowe in Buckinghamshire and Stourhead in Wiltshire, to tiny gems like the town gardens at Mompesson House, Salisbury, and Fenton House in Hampstead.

When the National Trust was founded in 1895, gardens were not part of its original brief of properties of 'natural beauty or historic interest'. Most of the great gardens were safely in the hands of families or institutions who had the staffs to maintain them. The kind of gardens beloved by the Victorians, with borders of tender plants and complex parterres, vegetable and fruit gardens, hothouses and conservatories, were labour intensive. At Petworth in Sussex in 1900, for instance, the Egremonts employed a garden staff of 25.

When gardens did begin to come to the National Trust, this labour intensity was one of the major problems to be faced, for the National Trust had neither the staff nor the funds to employ such staff. We have given the number of staff currently employed for each garden in this Handbook. This is to give you some indication of the scale of the garden and the time which you might spend looking around. But it also indicates how the National Trust is coping with gardens that once boasted many gardeners, somehow keeping them going with what the National Trust's first Gardens Adviser, Graham Stuart Thomas, used to call 'slender staff'. Petworth, with its staff of 25 in 1900, is now run with the help of 4 full-time gardeners. Of course, technical and labour-saving developments have helped, but the National Trust's gardening staff have also to give much thought to ways of eliminating non-essentials and cutting down on laborious tasks without detriment to the gardens themselves.

As great historic houses came to the National Trust, so did their gardens, beginning with Montacute in Somerset in 1931. With the establishment of the Country Houses Scheme in 1936, it was clear that more gardens were on their way, and Wightwick, Blickling, West Wycombe, Wallington and Powis Castle duly followed. But what of important gardens in their own right?

On 25 November 1947 a meeting was convened at the National Trust's head office at the instance of the President of the Royal Horticultural Society, Lord Aberconway, at which he proposed that a joint committee should be formed to raise money and administer a select few of the very best gardens in England, Wales and Northern Ireland. As a result of his initiative, the National Trust gained many gardens of great importance, including Major Lawrence Johnston's famous Gloucestershire garden, Hidcote Manor, and Lord Aberconway's own garden at Bodnant in North Wales. Mount Stewart in County Down, Nymans in Sussex and the Arboretum at Winkworth in Surrey were early results of the activities of the Gardens Committee.

One of the first members of the Gardens Committee was Vita Sackville-West, who initiated the National Trust's involvement with the National Gardens Scheme. The Queen's Institute for District Nurses was being wound up in 1948 to be incorporated into the new National Health Service. One of its very successful fund-raising efforts had been the opening of private gardens to the public on specified weekends during the summer months. Now some of the funds from this scheme were assigned to help the

National Trust with the care of its gardens. This scheme continues still and in 1993 the National Trust received £250,000, which the Gardens Panel, the modern successor of the Gardens Committee, assigned to a variety of projects.

At the launch of the National Trust's Gardens Year at the Royal Horticultural Hall in London in October 1990, I likened the management of the National Trust's gardens to a long-running soap opera. Occasionally – certainly more occasionally than in some 'soaps' – moments of high drama occur. One such was the terrible storm that overtook Southern England in the autumn of 1987, causing particular devastation to gardens like Nymans, Emmetts, Sheffield Park and Polesden Lacey. More storms struck in the early part of 1990, this time devastating the West Country and South Wales as well as revisiting Southern England. Killerton and Lanhydrock were both victims of this attack. The extent to which this devastation is no longer apparent speaks volumes for the dedication and skill of the Trust's gardeners.

Other moments of drama are kinder. In 1989 an anonymous benefactor put up £2 million to save the great landscape garden at Stowe in Buckinghamshire. The enormous task of keeping the classical buildings, lakes and general fabric of the garden in repair was proving too much for Stowe School, despite valiant efforts since taking over the garden in 1923. With such an enormous and important layout to renew, and with so many temples to restore, further funds will be needed. If Stowe epitomises the Augustan age, Biddulph Grange in Staffordshire represents High Victorian gardening at its remarkable peak. Biddulph, too, has been the subject of a major national appeal for £800,000 and visitors can, for the first time, enjoy this garden as it is gradually brought back to life. But these moments of high drama are the exception: most National Trust gardens evolve almost imperceptibly, so that the visitor can return again and again to enjoy familiar features. Now the Trust has acquired Prior Park, comparable with Stowe, with its unparalleled view over Bath. In order to restore Alexander Pope's 'wilderness' garden, as well as the more familiar parts of Ralph Allen's masterpiece, the Trust has launched an appeal for £400,000.

Our research tells us that gardens are one of the National Trust's greatest attractions: the most popular of all properties, Fountains Abbey and Studley Royal in Yorkshire, attracted 285,000 visitors in

1993. This was followed by Stourhead in Wiltshire with 251,830 visitors, Sissinghurst and its Kentish neighbour, Chartwell, with over 170,000 visitors each, and Hidcote and Sheffield Park with about 140,000 apiece. Landscape gardens like Studley Royal, Stourhead and Sheffield Park can, in the main, cope with large numbers of visitors, but some of the smaller gardens are less resilient. Not only does the pressure of large numbers wear out paths and lawns, but it is a less enjoyable experience to savour the serene splendours of Sissinghurst, Hidcote or Tintinhull in Somerset cheek by jowl with a crowd. In this Handbook, therefore, we have tried to warn you when to expect crowds and to vary your visiting to other times when the garden can be just as attractive and interesting. At Sissinghurst, where crowding was beginning to affect the pleasure of the visit, the Trust has decided to limit the number of people in the garden at any one time by means of a timed ticket system.

Surveys also show that of all properties, it is our gardens that attract *visitors* as opposed to National Trust *members* and that these visitors are highly likely to return. So we have provided calendars to recommend good times to visit gardens in all season. Of course, we hope that visitors will become members, to help to make this huge enterprise prosper and flourish for the enjoyment of future generations.

Enjoy your visits!

D. J. SALES
Chief Gardens Adviser

How to use this Handbook

THIS HANDBOOK is divided into nine sections: South-West England; Southern England; Wales and the Welsh Borders; London, Thames Valley and Chilterns; Heart of England; Eastern Counties; North-West England; North-East England and Northern Ireland. Within these sections the entries are arranged in alphabetical order giving postal address and telephone number whenever possible. General details of the garden are followed by a section giving information on visitor facilities at the property. To help you plan your itinerary we have provided, at the end of each entry, a list of other gardens in the area which you may wish to visit. The location of the gardens is shown on maps covering each of the nine areas and each entry contains details of the exact location together with a grid reference.

Opening times and admission fees

As this is not an annual publication we have not included detailed admission information – such as opening times and prices – as this varies from year to year. Instead we have simply stated whether the garden is open all year or for a limited period. We suggest you consult *The National Trust Handbook* which covers all National Trust properties open to the public and gives practical information on all aspects of visiting National Trust properties. This is published annually, issued free to all National Trust members, but is also sold to non-members in National Trust shops and high street bookshops (1996 edition £4.50). National Trust members should note that when a Trust garden is open under the National Gardens Scheme (see p.6), they may have to pay admission fees.

Visitors with disabilities

Where relevant, we have given information on access for people with severe mobility impairment to the gardens included in this Handbook. Several properties now have motorised buggies to ease access for disabled and infirm visitors and this, together with other appropriate information, is included in relevant entries under *Facilities for Disabled Visitors*. As a general rule, guide dogs for the blind and hearing dogs for the deaf are welcomed. Special features which may be of interest to visually impaired visitors, such as scented plants, are also mentioned in relevant entries. Although these details are correct at going to press we advise disabled visitors to contact the property beforehand to ensure the best visit possible.

Enquiries

Where possible telephone numbers have been given so that you can contact a property in advance if you have any specific queries regarding your visit. National Trust regional offices will also be able to help and a list of these showing the counties which they cover is given on pages 145–6.

Dogs

With the exception of guide dogs and hearing dogs the National Trust regrets that dogs are not admitted to its gardens.

Membership of the National Trust

Membership subscriptions are an increasingly vital source of the National Trust's income. If you join the National Trust you will contribute to its conservation work and the protection of its gardens, historic buildings and outstanding countryside. You will also gain free entry to most properties in its care, and each year will receive the members' Handbook, three colour magazines, a mail order catalogue, the annual report and two regional newsletters. For details of subscription rates and a membership leaflet please contact the National Trust Membership Department, PO Box 39, Bromley, Kent BR1 3XL (tel. 0181–464 1111).

THE GARDENS

South-West England

CORNWALL · DEVON · DORSET · SOMERSET

Antony

Torpoint, Cornwall PL11 2QA Tel: Plymouth (01752) 812191

SOIL & TERRAIN: lime-free soil. Sloping site
ALTITUDE: 30m (100ft)
GARDENERS: four

SPECIAL FEATURES: NCCPG National Collection of day lilies. Topiary

Early 18th-century house in superb setting above Tamar estuary. Landscape setting shows influence of Humphry Repton who produced one of his first Red Books for this site. Lawns sweep down to the Tamar and are edged to the west with clipped yew hedges. Topiary includes tall wigwam shape. Wall of old kitchen garden bordered by espaliered fruit trees and row of magnolias. Sheltered flower garden beyond yew hedge provides colourful summer display and terraces are planted with roses. Garden also features a knot garden planted with box and germander. Grounds include fine specimen trees such as ginkgo and cork oak.

BEST TIMES TO VISIT: Summer for colour in garden
SEASON: April to end October
ROUTES: Free wandering throughout grounds. Paths in garden
FACILITIES: Tea-room, shop, WCs
FACILITIES FOR DISABLED VISITORS: Garden largely accessible to wheelchair users
LOCATION: 5m W of Plymouth via Torpoint car ferry, 2m NW of Torpoint, N of A374, 16m SE of Liskeard, 15m E of Looe [201:SX418564]
OTHER GARDENS IN AREA: Saltram, Cotehele, Mount Edgcumbe (not NT)

Arlington Court

Arlington, nr Barnstaple, Devon EX31 4LP
Tel: Barnstaple (01271) 850296

SOIL & TERRAIN: light, acid soil overlying slate. Flat and exposed to wind, very wet
ALTITUDE: 243m (800ft)
GARDENERS: two
SPECIAL FEATURES: ponds, conservatory, rhododendrons, Victorian garden, cast iron pergola, *Fraxinus* planting

Thirty-acre garden of Georgian house in parkland setting with lawns, wilderness pond, spring bulbs and wild flowers. Also collection of recently planted species of *Fraxinus*. Formal one-acre Victorian garden consisting of herbaceous beds and annual borders with raised circular beds and a conservatory. Garden and house given to NT in 1949 by the owner, Miss Rosalie Chichester.

BEST TIMES TO VISIT: May to June for rhododendrons. June to September for Victorian garden and borders. Throughout season for woodland walks and carriage rides (subject to availability)
SEASON: April to end October
PUBLICATIONS: Guidebook for house and garden
ROUTES: Formal and informal paths in garden with additional access through park to lake and wooded river valley
FACILITIES: Restaurant, self-service area, shop, WCs, car park
FACILITIES FOR DISABLED VISITORS: Wheelchair access but many gravel paths. Wheelchair available. ♿ WC. Guide dogs admitted. Scented plants and textured tree bark
LOCATION: 8m E of Barnstaple on A39 [180:SS611405]
OTHER GARDENS IN AREA: Knightshayes Court, Marwood Hill (not NT), Rosemoor (not NT)

Buckland Abbey

Yelverton, Devon PL20 6EY Tel: Yelverton (01822) 853607

SOIL & TERRAIN: acid soil. Sloping terrain on SW, fairly sheltered site
ALTITUDE: 75m (250ft)
GARDENERS: one

Garden of 3½ acres, largely of 20th-century creation, with shrub and herb gardens, but contains a very old yew walk to the north of the Abbey, badly damaged by storms in 1990. The south-west elevation is wreathed in climbers, with the south elevation dominated by two vast magnolias. The herb garden was probably established after a visit by Vita Sackville-West. The irregularly shaped dwarf box-hedged beds contain over 50 different herbs.

BEST TIMES TO VISIT: Spring for camellias and rhododendrons
SEASON: All year
PUBLICATIONS: Herb garden leaflet. Section in Book of the House
ROUTES: Free wandering and countryside walks
PLANT SALES: Herbs only
FACILITIES: Restaurant, WCs, shop, craft workshops, car park
FACILITIES FOR DISABLED VISITORS: Wheelchair access although return journey to car park not easy. Motorised buggy. Wheelchair available. Guide dogs admitted. Braille leaflet
LOCATION: 6m S of Tavistock, 11m N of Plymouth. Turn off A386 ¼m S of Yelverton [201:SX487667]
OTHER GARDENS IN AREA: Saltram, The Garden House (not NT) at Buckland Monachorum, Cotehele, Antony

Castle Drogo

Drewsteignton, Devon EX6 6PB Tel: Chagford (01647) 433306

SOIL & TERRAIN: acid, thin and stony soil. Rugged and exposed terrain
ALTITUDE: 305m (1000ft)
GARDENERS: two

SPECIAL FEATURES: formal design, herbaceous borders, rose garden, shrubs, yew hedges, rhododendrons and azaleas

Twelve-acre garden created by Julius Drewe, the owner, and Edwin Lutyens, his architect, in 1920s. Lutyens designed a formal garden enclosed by yew hedges north of the drive, with planting devised by George Dillistone. Main garden consists of series of formal terraces. First contains rectangular rose beds of modern cultivars to withstand the weather in these bleak surroundings. At corners of first terrace, arbours of *Parrotia persica* surrounded yew hedges linked by serpentine path of Indian pattern (influenced by

Lutyens's work in New Delhi) and herbaceous borders. Steps lead to second terrace of borders and centre beds containing various herbs. More steps to shrub borders designed by Dillistone in 1927. Sloping path to huge circular lawn surrounded by tall yew hedge, originally laid for tennis but now used for croquet. Below, steps lead to rhododendron dell and then to Chapel Garden and house.

BEST TIMES TO VISIT: Summer when herbaceous borders and roses at their best
SEASON: April to end October
PUBLICATIONS: Garden leaflet
ROUTES: Free wandering on paths throughout garden
PLANT SALES: NT Enterprises plant centre
FACILITIES: Restaurant, tea-room, WCs, shop, car park
FACILITIES FOR DISABLED VISITORS: Wheelchair access to garden. Wheelchair available. ♿ WC
LOCATION: 4m S of A30 Exeter–Okehampton via Crockernwell [191:SX721900]
OTHER GARDENS IN AREA: Buckland Abbey, Killerton

Coleton Fishacre Garden

Coleton, Kingswear, Dartmouth, Devon TQ6 0EQ
Tel: Kingswear (01803) 752466

SOIL & TERRAIN: acid, light soil. Mostly frost-free, sheltered, mild with undulating terrain
ALTITUDE: 100m (330ft)
GARDENERS: two

SPECIAL FEATURES: Lutyens-influenced formal terraces. Gazebo. Range of unusual and tender plants and exotic shrubs: bamboos, Dawn Redwood, Chilean myrtle and Swamp Cypress

Twenty-acre garden surrounding a Lutyens-styled house. Formal terraces and walled garden situated in a stream-fed valley with ponds. Spectacular coastal scenery. Garden created by Lady D'Oyly Carte between 1926–40, in overgrown and overmature state when acquired by the NT in 1982. Planted with range of uncommon trees, tender and exotic shrubs – many from the southern hemisphere which thrive in the mild, sheltered and relatively frost-free environment. During restoration the garden is being carefully improved and plant collection expanded in line with the special botanic character of the property.

BEST TIMES TO VISIT: March to May for rhododendrons, camellias, magnolias, bulbs and spring wild flowers. June to August for formal terraces, rill garden and beds
SEASON: April to end October
PUBLICATIONS: Pamphlet with garden plan
ROUTES: Free wandering in designated areas
PLANT SALES: Occasional small plant sale of surplus plants propagated for the garden. Unusual range when available, but in limited numbers
FACILITIES: WCs, car park, light refreshments at peak times
FACILITIES FOR DISABLED VISITORS: Limited wheelchair access and for visitors using crutches owing to undulating nature of terrain
LOCATION: 2m from Kingswear. Take Lower Ferry road, turn off at tollhouse and signposted [202:SX910508]
OTHER GARDENS IN AREA: Overbecks, Compton Castle, Saltram, Killerton, Dartington Hall (not NT)

Cotehele

St Dominick, nr Saltash PL12 6TA Tel: Liskeard (01579) 50434

SOIL & TERRAIN: lime-free soil. Sloping site to River Tamar
ALTITUDE: 75m (250ft)
GARDENERS: three
SPECIAL FEATURES: exotic and tender plants

Cotehele House, built by the Edgcumbe family in the late 15th century, stands at the head of a steep valley with woodland sheltering the valley garden. Exotic and tender plants, such as palms, ferns and *Gunnera manicata*, thrive in the mild climate. Fine display of rhododendrons and azaleas. Further down the valley are spruces, hemlocks and larches. Garden contains the medieval stewpond, now filled with water-lilies, and a domed dovecote. Areas of garden surrounding the house are more formal. 19th-century terraces with roses and magnolias to the east of house. North-west of house is a meadow with Judas trees and daffodils.

BEST TIMES TO VISIT: Spring for daffodils, Judas trees and magnolias. May to June for rhododendrons and azaleas
SEASON: All year
PUBLICATIONS: Section in Book of the House. Garden guide
ROUTES: Free wandering throughout garden
PLANT SALES: Extensive plant centre
FACILITIES: Restaurant, shop, WCs
FACILITIES FOR DISABLED VISITORS: Garden unsuitable because of steep slope and gravel paths. ♿ WC. Guide dogs admitted
LOCATION: 1m W of Calstock, 8m SW of Tavistock [201:SX422685]
OTHER GARDENS IN AREA: Antony, Saltram

Dunster Castle

Dunster, nr Minehead, Somerset TA24 6SL
Tel: Dunster (01643) 821314

SOIL & TERRAIN: acid, light soil. Very steep terrain. Exposed to N and S. Microclimate
ALTITUDE: 60m (200ft)
GARDENERS: three
SPECIAL FEATURES: citrus collection. NCCPG National Collection of Arbutus. Camellias, magnolias and sun-loving plants. Conservatory

Seventeen-acre steep wooded garden surrounding Dunster Castle. Earliest account described by James Savage in 1830 when the tor was covered with evergreens and flowering trees and shrubs. The south-east slopes and terraces offer conditions suitable for tender sun-loving plants which include a 100-year-old lemon tree. The Mill Walk at the base of the tor was mostly planted by the late Mrs Alys Luttrell in the early 1920s and restored by the NT after receiving the property from Col Sir Walter Luttrell in 1976.

BEST TIMES TO VISIT: May to July for camellias and magnolias. Try to avoid Bank Holidays and July and August
SEASON: February to end October
PUBLICATIONS: Garden leaflet
ROUTES: Free wandering throughout the garden
FACILITIES: Shop, WCs, refreshments in Dunster village

FACILITIES FOR DISABLED VISITORS: ♿ WC. Guide dogs admitted. Scented plants: mock orange, rosemary, orange
LOCATION: 3m E of Minehead on A396 just off A39 [181:ST995435]
OTHER GARDENS IN AREA: Knightshayes, Combe Sydenham (not NT), Cannington College gardens (not NT)

Glendurgan

Helford River, Mawnan Smith, nr Falmouth, Cornwall TR11 5JZ
Tel: Bodmin (01208) 74281 (enquiries)

SOIL & TERRAIN: lime-free. Terrain slopes steeply towards Helford River
ALTITUDE: 30m (100ft)
GARDENERS: three
SPECIAL FEATURES: laurel maze. Spring shrubs and flowers. Holy Corner and rare trees

Informal 28-acre woodland garden at head of steep valley leading to Helford River. Garden originally planned by Alfred Fox, owner of prosperous local shipping company in 1820s and 1830s who planted garden with exotic plants brought back from the Americas, Africa, Far East and the Antipodes. Planted laurel maze and two tulip trees which are over 150 years old. Next two generations of the family expanded the garden and planted many trees including cedars, weeping spruce, cypresses, and tree ferns. Rhododendrons, camellias, magnolias and hydrangeas provide colour as do the carpets of primroses, bluebells, primulas and columbines beneath the trees in spring. A Holy Corner is planted with trees and shrubs with Biblical associations – a yew, tree of thorns and tree of heaven.

BEST TIMES TO VISIT: March for magnolias. April to May for rhododendrons and primroses, bluebells and primulas. Autumn for leaf colour
SEASON: March to end October
PUBLICATIONS: Cornish Gardens colour souvenir. Garden guide
ROUTES: Winding paths throughout garden
FACILITIES: WC, shop, car park, light refreshments
FACILITIES FOR DISABLED VISITORS: Garden slopes steeply so unsuitable for wheelchairs. Scented plants. Guide dogs admitted

LOCATION: 4m SW of Falmouth, ½m SW of Mawnan Smith, on road to Helford Passage [204:SW772277]
OTHER GARDENS IN AREA: St Michael's Mount, Trelissick

Killerton

Broadclyst, Exeter, Devon EX5 3LE Tel: Exeter (01392) 881345

SOIL & TERRAIN: acid, sandy soil. Sloping hillside, with steeper upper slopes. S-facing, sheltered site

ALTITUDE: 60.9m (200ft)
GARDENERS: four

The 17 acres of Killerton Garden were first laid out by Sir Thomas Acland, 7th Baronet, and his agent, John Veitch, when the house was rebuilt in 1777. Later, Veitch founded a famous firm of nurserymen which sent plant hunters (including the Lobb brothers and Ernest Wilson) all over the world to bring back new species. Many of these found a home in Killerton Garden. The garden was developed by successive generations of the Acland family and the connection with Veitch continued into the present century. In the 1920s Sir Francis Acland, 14th Baronet, supported Captain Kingdon-Ward's plant-hunting expeditions to the Himalayas, which brought new rhododendron species to Killerton. In the early 1900s the herbaceous borders were laid out by William Robinson.

BEST TIMES TO VISIT: February and March for spring flowers and magnolias. April to June for rhododendrons. May and June for wild flowers. June to September for herbaceous borders
PUBLICATIONS: Garden guide leaflet
ROUTES: Free wandering
PLANT SALES: NT Enterprises when property open to the public
FACILITIES: Restaurant, tea-room, WCs, shop, car park
FACILITIES FOR DISABLED VISITORS: Wheelchair access. Wheelchair available. Three motorised buggies. Guide dogs admitted
LOCATION: 7m N of Exeter, entrance off B3185 [192:SX9700]
OTHER GARDENS IN AREA: Knightshayes Court, Castle Drogo

Kingston Lacy

Wimborne Minster, Dorset BH21 4EA
Tel: Wimborne (01202) 883402

SOIL & TERRAIN: light soil mix, very chalky. Flat terrain
ALTITUDE: 25m (85ft)
GARDENERS: three permanent; one seasonal, one trainee

Two hundred and fifty acres of parkland with prize-winning herd of Red Devon cattle surrounding 17th-century house designed by Sir Roger Pratt. Landscaping dates from the 18th century with 13 acres of formal garden and woodland walks. Garden overgrown when acquired by the NT and extensive restoration has taken place, particularly in the Victorian fernery, which contains over 20 species, and in the sunken garden. Trees include magnificent cedars of Lebanon some of which were planted by visiting royalty, including Kaiser Wilhelm and Queen Mary. Rhododendron and azalea walk. Shady lime avenue. Snowdrop viewing in season. Dutch parterre and croquet lawn. Egyptian obelisk.

BEST TIMES TO VISIT: May to June for rhododendrons and azaleas. All season for parkland and trees
SEASON: April to end October
PUBLICATIONS: Section in property guidebook. Free map issued to visitors outlining routes and features
ROUTES: Routes around garden shown on free map
PLANT SALES: Herbs and heathers usually on sale
FACILITIES: Restaurant, tea-room, WCs, shop
FACILITIES FOR DISABLED VISITORS: Motorised buggy. Wheelchair access but some steep and deep gravel paths. ♿ WC. Guide dogs admitted. Textured tree bark
LOCATION: On B3082 Wimborne–Blandford road, 1½m W of Wimborne [195:SY980019]
OTHER GARDENS IN AREA: Compton Acres (not NT), Cranborne Manor Gardens (not NT)

Knightshayes Gardens

Bolham, Tiverton, Devon EX16 7RG
Tel: Tiverton (01884) 254665 (admin)/253264 (gardens)

SOIL & TERRAIN: fertile rich reddish acid to neutral Devon soil overlaying sandstone shale. Undulating terrain. Mild SW prevailing winds

ALTITUDE: 136m (450ft)

GARDENERS: six including estate staff and propagator

Fifty acres of mid 20th-century gardens overlay the original 4-acre Victorian garden and include the development of surrounding woodland areas. Created by Joyce, Lady Heathcoat Amory and the late Sir John who together designed, planted and maintained this garden until 1971 when given to the NT. Topiary chase scene, battlemented yew enclosure surrounding water-lily pool. Unusual trees, shrubs, bulbs and herbaceous plants, 'Garden in Wood'. The NT Plant Conservation Unit (not open to the public) accepts gifts of rare seed and young plants from around the world to be grown on for distribution to other NT gardens.

BEST TIMES TO VISIT: April to May for rhododendrons and spring flowers. Summer for herbaceous borders. Autumn colours. Visitors disperse within gardens easily. Bank Holidays sometimes busy

SEASON: April to end October

PUBLICATIONS: Garden guide including map

ROUTES: Free wandering on gravel and grass paths and all year through woodland on Impey Walk

PLANT SALES: NT Enterprises plant sales in Garden Shop. Wide range of plants for sale (often those not found in garden centres). Open March until Christmas

FACILITIES: Restaurant, WCs, shop

FACILITIES FOR DISABLED VISITORS: Wheelchair access but some steep gradients. Wheelchair available. Guide dogs admitted

LOCATION: 2m N of Tiverton (A396), 8m from M5 jnt 27 [181:SS960151]

OTHER GARDENS IN AREA: Killerton, Arlington Court, Dunster Castle

Lanhydrock

Bodmin, Cornwall PL30 5AD Tel: Bodmin (01208) 73320

SOIL & TERRAIN: lime-free soil. Valley site
ALTITUDE: 121m (400ft)
GARDENERS: four full-time; one part-time

Thirty acres of gardens surround 19th-century granite house built to replace original 17th-century house largely destroyed by fire. Formal gardens to the front of the house also date from 19th century and feature geometrically shaped beds of roses interspersed with clipped yews. Terraces feature beds of annuals edged by box. Also an unusual herbaceous circular bed within a boundary of yew which has a flowering season from April to October. Garden features the NCCPG National Collection of crocosmias. Beyond the parapet of the walled garden lies a more informal area on the steep slopes rising above the house. This includes large Himalayan magnolias, rhododendrons, camellias and a stream edged with primulas, astilbes, arums, rodgersias and other water-loving plants. Surrounding woodland was badly damaged by the 1990 storms.

BEST TIMES TO VISIT: April to May for rhododendrons and spring flowering shrubs. Summer for herbaceous borders, hydrangeas, crocosmias and roses
SEASON: All year
PUBLICATIONS: Section in Book of the House. Garden guide
ROUTES: Gravel paths through formal garden. Wild garden features winding paths for free wandering
PLANT SALES: NT nursery at Lanhydrock supplies plant centre which specialises in plants seen at NT Cornish gardens, including many rare rhododendrons
FACILITIES: Shop, restaurant, WCs
FACILITIES FOR DISABLED VISITORS: Formal garden has some gravel paths and a few steps. Wild garden is on slope so difficult for wheelchairs. ♿ WC
LOCATION: 2½m SE of Bodmin [200:SX085636]
OTHER GARDENS IN AREA: Trerice, Cotehele, Trewithen (not NT), Pencarrow House and Gardens (not NT), Tregrehan (not NT)

Lytes Cary Manor

Charlton Mackrell, Somerton, Somerset TA11 7HU

SOIL & TERRAIN: heavy, limy soil. Level terrain
ALTITUDE: 60.9m (200ft)
GARDENERS: one, plus tenant
SPECIAL FEATURES: Elizabethan-style garden

Charming Somerset manor house inhabited by the Lyte family from 13th to 18th centuries. Henry Lyte's *Niewe Herball* – a translation from the work of a Flemish herbalist – was dedicated to Queen Elizabeth I. Neglected after the Lyte family left in 1748 but rescued from decay by Sir Walter Jenner who bought the house and grounds early this century. Sir Walter created a wonderful Elizabethan-style garden with clipped yew hedges dividing areas of the garden. Colourful herbaceous border with urns. Raised walk overlooking orchard planted with crab apples, medlars and quinces. Yew-hedged alley leading to formal pool with statue of Flora and Diana. Hornbeam tunnel. Border along south front stocked with species contemporary with *Niewe Herball.*

BEST TIMES TO VISIT: Summer for vivid colour in herbaceous border
SEASON: April to end October
PUBLICATIONS: Section in guidebook to property
ROUTES: Free wandering throughout garden
PLANT SALES: Plant centre selling interesting and unusual locally grown plants
FACILITIES FOR DISABLED VISITORS: Garden accessible to wheelchairs. Scented plants in herbaceous borders. Guide dogs admitted
LOCATION: 1m N of Ilchester bypass A303 [183:ST529269]
OTHER GARDENS IN AREA: Tintinhull House, Montacute, Stourhead, Milton Lodge Gardens (not NT), Melbury House (not NT), East Lambrook Manor (not NT), Hadspen House (not NT), Barrington Court

Montacute House

Montacute, Somerset TA15 6XP Tel: Martock (01935) 823289

SOIL & TERRAIN: limy soil. Level terrain
ALTITUDE: 75m (250ft)
GARDENERS: three full-time; one trainee
SPECIAL FEATURES: raised walks. Old shrub roses. Colourful borders. Monterey cypress

Garden of this late Elizabethan house follows outlines of the original layout but with 19th- and 20th-century additions. Raised walks frame a sunken lawn encircled with clipped yew and thorn with a 19th-century pond at its centre. Borders of shrub roses under the retaining wall include species grown in the 16th century such as *Rosa gallica officinalis* and *R.* 'Alba Maxima' planted with the advice of Vita Sackville-West. Mrs Reiss from nearby Tintinhull decided on the strong colour schemes for the border in the entrance court which includes herbaceous perennials, standard honeysuckles, clematis and vines and contrasts well with the soft honey-coloured stone of the house. The west drive, created in 1851, is lined with trees and fronted by clipped Irish yews. Surrounding estate and park has several waymarked walks.

BEST TIMES TO VISIT: Summer for border colour and roses
SEASON: All year (closed Tuesdays)
PUBLICATIONS: Section in Book of the House. Garden leaflet. Also leaflets detailing park walks
ROUTES: Paths in the garden. Suggested walks in surrounding woods and parkland detailed in leaflets
PLANT SALES: Plant centre selling interesting and unusual locally grown plants open April to end September. Also herb barrow sales
FACILITIES: Restaurant, WCs, shop
FACILITIES FOR DISABLED VISITORS: Garden accessible for wheelchair users. Guide dogs admitted. ♿WC
LOCATION: In Montacute village, 4m W of Yeovil, on S side of A3088, 3m E of A303 near Ilchester [183 & 193:ST499172]
OTHER GARDENS IN AREA: Tintinhull, East Lambrook Manor (not NT), Lytes Cary, Barrington Court

Overbecks

Sharpitor, Salcombe, Devon TQ8 8LW
Tel: Salcombe (0154 884) 2893 or 3238 (evenings)

SOIL & TERRAIN: alkaline, light soil. Steeply sloping in parts and mostly terraced. Sheltered, high above sea level
ALTITUDE: 30m (100ft)
GARDENERS: two

SPECIAL FEATURES: exotic and unusual tender plants, trees and shrubs, citrus trees in conservatory, bananas, palms, camphor tree, echiums, *Beschorneria yuccoides*, herbaceous borders and statue. *Magnolia campbellii* (planted 1901)

Created in 20th century and left to the NT in 1937 by Mr Otto Overbecks. Considered by many to be the nearest to a Mediterranean garden owned by the NT. Situated on steep hillside with spectacular views across Salcombe Estuary. Mild microclimate gives ideal conditions for growth of rare/tender plants such as palms, camphor trees, bananas. Unlike many West Country gardens does not rely on rhododendrons and camellias because of alkaline soil. In summer herbaceous garden is a blaze of colour. Small parterre recently created where citrus plants stand during summer. Pots and urns containing agaves are also placed around the garden to continue the Mediterranean theme. The old and famous *Magnolia campbellii* is a delight not to be missed in early spring.

BEST TIMES TO VISIT: Mid February to March for magnolia. July to August for herbaceous garden at most colourful
SEASON: All year
PUBLICATIONS: Garden guide with plan
ROUTES: Free wandering throughout garden
FACILITIES: Tea-room, WC, shop (April to October), car park
FACILITIES FOR DISABLED VISITORS: Wheelchair available (strong pusher needed). Some scented plants eg curry plant, pineapple-scented salvia, *Cosmos atrosanguineus* (chocolate scent)
LOCATION: 1½m SW of Salcombe, signposted from Malborough and Salcombe, narrow, single-track lanes [202:SX728374]
OTHER GARDENS IN AREA: Saltram House, Coleton Fishacre, Dartington Hall (not NT)

St Michael's Mount

Marazion, Cornwall TR17 0HT Tel: Penzance (01736) 710507

SOIL & TERRAIN: light soil overlying granite. Steep, very exposed site
ALTITUDE: 18m (60ft)
GARDENERS: three

SPECIAL FEATURES: shrubs, rare cactus, rock plants. Sub-tropical plants: *Sparmannia africana*, blue African lilies

Terraced rock garden and 18th-century walled garden dominated by medieval castle. Rare and interesting tropical and sub-tropical plants and shrubs. Native wild flowers grow in the grounds. Few would expect any kind of garden to flourish on this inhospitable rocky island exposed to gales from the sea. Garden remains property of the St Aubyn family and is not owned by the NT.

BEST TIMES TO VISIT: April to May
SEASON: All year (tide and weather permitting)
PUBLICATIONS: Garden plan and information available on request
ROUTES: Free wandering
PLANT SALES: Limited plant sales during summer
FACILITIES: WCs, restaurant, shop (April to end October)
FACILITIES FOR DISABLED VISITORS: Not suitable for wheelchairs due to the very steep site and cobbled paths
LOCATION: ½m S of A394 at Marazion. Access on foot over causeway at low tide. Ferry at high tide during summer months
OTHER GARDENS IN AREA: Trengwainton, Trelissick, Glendurgan

Saltram

Plympton, Plymouth, Devon PL7 3UH
Tel: Plymouth (01752) 336546

SOIL & TERRAIN: acid, light soil. Undulating hilltop site. Some parts exposed to SW

ALTITUDE: 30m (100ft)
GARDENERS: two

Twenty-acre garden dates from 1770 but was altered to its present design in the 19th century. The beautiful Lime Walk is a particular delight during spring with old cultivars of narcissus and in autumn with *Cyclamen hederifolium*. In the central glade there are some superb trees including the stone pine and Monterey pine. The various walks are bordered by specimen trees and shrubs, magnolias, camellias, many rhododendrons and Japanese maples being of particular note. To extend the flowering period recent plantings have included *Hypericum*, hydrangeas, *Indigofera*, buddlejas and fuchsias. Orangery (citrus trees moved outside in summer).

BEST TIMES TO VISIT: Spring for magnolias, camellias and narcissi. Autumn for cyclamen in flower and leaf colour
PUBLICATIONS: Leaflet with plan
ROUTES: Free wandering
FACILITIES: Restaurant, tea-room, WCs, shop, car park
FACILITIES FOR DISABLED VISITORS: Wheelchair access. Wheelchair available. Guide dogs admitted. Scented plants
LOCATION: 3½m E of Plymouth city centre, take Plympton turn from Marsh Mills roundabout [201:SX520557]
OTHER GARDENS IN AREA: Buckland Abbey, Antony, Cotehele

Tintinhull House Garden

Tintinhull, nr Yeovil, Somerset BA22 9PZ
Tel: Yeovil (01935) 822545

SOIL & TERRAIN: neutral soil. Level terrain
ALTITUDE: 30m (100ft)
GARDENERS: one full-time; one part-time
SPECIAL FEATURES: striking planting schemes

Tintinhull House Garden is a tiny, delightful walled garden divided into separate areas by clipped hedges. Garden largely the inspiration of Mrs Phyllis Reiss who moved to Tintinhull in 1933. Domes of box line the central path leading from the west front of the 17th-century house (not open) to the different 'rooms', including an azalea garden, a fountain garden planted with white-flowering and silver plants around a central pool and a kitchen garden with espaliered fruit trees and paths edged with catmint. The more formal pool garden features a rectangular pool flanked with long beds carefully planned for flower and foliage effects. The east-facing bed contains a vivid colour scheme of yellows, oranges and scarlet, while the opposite bed features contrasting pastel colours. Closer to the house stands the impressive cedar court dominated by a cedar of Lebanon with borders showing a striking mix of plum- and gold-foliaged flowers and shrubs.

BEST TIMES TO VISIT: Ingenious planting provides interest throughout season
SEASON: April to end September
PUBLICATIONS: Guidebook and detailed plantlist available
ROUTES: Paths throughout garden
FACILITIES: Refreshments in courtyard. WC
FACILITIES FOR DISABLED VISITORS: Wheelchair available. Some steps in garden but most areas accessible to wheelchair users. Guide dogs admitted. Roses, honeysuckles and other scented plants
LOCATION: 5m NW of Yeovil, ½m S of A303 on E outskirts of Tintinhull [183:ST503198]
OTHER GARDENS IN AREA: Montacute, Lytes Cary, East Lambrook Manor (not NT), Hadspen House (not NT), Barrington Court

Trelissick

Feock, nr Truro, Cornwall TR3 6QL Tel: Truro (01872) 862090

SOIL & TERRAIN: lime-free soil. Sheltered valley garden
ALTITUDE: 30m (100ft)
GARDENERS: four
SPECIAL FEATURES: exotic species of plants and trees

Twenty-five-acre garden renowned for rich collection of species and hybrid rhododendrons including 'Trelissick Port Wine' and salmon. Also many rare varieties of hydrangea. Dell is planted with hydrangeas, rhododendrons and exotic plants including a banana, Chilean and Australian ferns. Fig garden. Beautiful Japanese cedar stands on lawn edged by herbaceous borders. Small walled garden with aromatic plants.

BEST TIMES TO VISIT: April to May for rhododendrons. Summer for hydrangeas. Something of interest throughout the year

SEASON: March to end October. Woodland walk also open November to end March
PUBLICATIONS: Cornish Gardens colour souvenir. Garden leaflet. Woodland walk leaflet
ROUTES: Free wandering throughout garden and woodland
PLANT SALES: Plant centre selling plants raised at the NT nursery at Lanhydrock. Specialises in plants on view at NT Cornish gardens, including rare species of rhododendrons
FACILITIES: Restaurant/tea-room, shop, WCs, gallery
FACILITIES FOR DISABLED VISITORS: Upper parts of garden accessible to wheelchair users but has loose gravel paths. Guide dogs admitted. Small walled garden with aromatic plants. ♿WC
LOCATION: 4m S of Truro on both sides of B3289 above King Harry Ferry [204:SW837396]
OTHER GARDENS IN AREA: Glendurgan, Trehane (not NT), Trebah (not NT), Chyverton (not NT), County Demonstration Garden at Probus (not NT)

Trengwainton

nr Penzance, Cornwall TR20 8RZ Tel: Penzance (01736) 63021

SOIL & TERRAIN: lime-free. Gently sloping terrain on either side of small valley running E towards sea
ALTITUDE: 75m (250ft)
GARDENERS: three
SPECIAL FEATURES: walled garden, stream garden

Created largely by Lt Col Sir Edward Bolitho who inherited the Victorian mansion and its grounds in 1925. Sheltered and well-watered garden rarely experiencing frosts. Excellent collection of tender and half-hardy trees, shrubs and other plants. Also traces of earlier garden including a walled garden, using the warmer brick rather than the local granite, with steeply sloping beds planted with vegetables and tender plants to get full benefit of sun. Walled garden also houses shrubs and trees needing extra protection – such as *Magnolia cylindrica* and *M. sprengeri diva* – while the borders are filled with plants including camellias, eucalyptus and *Azara dentata* (from Chile). The tender *Rhododendron macabeanum* and *R. elliottii* were raised from seed brought back from Kingdon-Ward's expedition to the eastern Himalayas in 1927. Australian tree ferns, hydrangeas, arum lilies and candelabra primulas edge the stream. Beautiful magnolia garden to the south of house including a huge specimen of *Magnolia sargentiana robusta*. Lawns to the front of the house give a magnificent view of the sea.

BEST TIMES TO VISIT: Good all year. March to May for impressive display of camellias, magnolias, rhododendrons and azaleas
SEASON: March to end October
PUBLICATIONS: Garden guide. Cornish Gardens colour souvenir
ROUTES: Free wandering throughout garden
PLANT SALES: Good selection of plants
FACILITIES: WCs, garden teas (not NT) weather permitting
FACILITIES FOR DISABLED VISITORS: Most parts of garden accessible to wheelchair users. Guide dogs admitted. ♿WC
LOCATION: 2m NW of Penzance, ½m W of Heamoor on Penzance–Morvah road (B3312) [203:SW445315]
OTHER GARDENS IN AREA: St Michael's Mount, Glendurgan Garden

Trerice

nr Newquay, Cornwall TR8 4PG Tel: Newquay (01637) 875404

SOIL & TERRAIN: limy soil. Level terrain
ALTITUDE: 30m (100ft)
GARDENERS: one
SPECIAL FEATURES: fruit trees planted in quincunx pattern

Small summer garden with enclosed courts, lawns and bowling green. Garden surrounds Elizabethan manor house but there are no surviving or reconstructed garden features from that period. Orchard of fruit trees planted in 17th-century quincunx pattern. Collection of perennials, climbers and shrubs. Back court with fuchsias, lonicera and roses. Front walled courtyard with herbaceous borders. Extraordinary collection of lawnmowers in hayloft of former stable.

BEST TIMES TO VISIT: Summer for herbaceous borders and roses. Autumn for fruit
SEASON: April to end October

PUBLICATIONS: Section in guide
ROUTES: Free wandering throughout garden
PLANT SALES: Small selection of plants
FACILITIES: Refreshments, shop, WCs
FACILITIES FOR DISABLED VISITORS: Most parts of garden accessible to wheelchair users. ♿ WC
LOCATION: 3m SE of Newquay via A392 and A3058 [200:SW841585]
OTHER GARDENS IN AREA: Chyverton (not NT), County Demonstration Garden at Probus (not NT), Trehane (not NT), Trewithen (not NT)

Southern England

HAMPSHIRE · KENT · SURREY · EAST AND WEST SUSSEX · WILTSHIRE

Bateman's

Burwash, Etchingham, East Sussex TN19 7DS
Tel: Burwash (01435) 882302

SOIL & TERRAIN: lime free. S-facing, sloping and level terrain
ALTITUDE: 75m (250ft)
GARDENERS: two
SPECIAL FEATURES: rose garden, herb border, pear alley, mulberry garden

Rudyard Kipling lived at Bateman's from 1902 until his death in 1936, writing some of his greatest works here including *Puck of Pook's Hill*, *If* and *The Glory of the Garden*. The Kiplings did much to create the peaceful garden which now surrounds the Jacobean house and planted hedges, laid out paths and planted the rose garden. Pear alley planted with old pears such as 'Winter Nelis' and 'Doyenné du Comice' trained to form a tunnel and interspersed with clematis. Shade-tolerant plants such as lily of the valley and Solomon's seal are planted underneath. Pond was designed for young children to use for swimming and boating. Mulberry garden has box-edged borders of shrubs and perennials, spring borders designed by Graham Thomas. Walk to mill house by the river is edged with cherries, amelanchier, wild flowers and spring bulbs.

BEST TIMES TO VISIT: Spring for wild garden and spring borders. Summer for rose and mulberry gardens
SEASON: April to end October
PUBLICATIONS: Section in property guidebook
ROUTES: Free wandering
FACILITIES: Tea-room, shop, WCs
FACILITIES FOR DISABLED VISITORS: Wheelchair access to garden with routes avoiding steps. ♿ WC
LOCATION: ½m S of Burwash (A265) [199:TQ671238]
OTHER GARDENS IN AREA: Scotney Castle, Sissinghurst

Chartwell

Westerham, Kent TN16 1PS Tel: Edenbridge (01732) 866368

SOIL & TERRAIN: medium loam over greensand. Hilltop garden dipping into valley
ALTITUDE: 121m (400ft)
GARDENERS: five full-time; one careership
SPECIAL FEATURES: rose garden. Attractive colour schemes

A garden planned by Sir Winston and Lady Churchill with terraced lawns, ponds, orchard and flower beds, in a pleasant country-garden style, enjoying fine views over the Weald of Kent. In 1958 a golden rose walk was created by their children to commemorate the Churchills' golden wedding.

BEST TIMES TO VISIT: Open all season. Try to avoid weekends and Bank Holidays
SEASON: April to end October
PUBLICATIONS: Section in property guidebook
ROUTES: Extensive paths throughout garden
FACILITIES: Restaurant/tea-room, WCs, shop
FACILITIES FOR DISABLED VISITORS: Wheelchair access to part of garden. Guide dogs admitted. Scented plants
LOCATION: 2m S of Westerham, fork left off B2026 after 1½m [188:TQ455515]
OTHER GARDENS IN AREA: Emmetts Garden, Quebec House, Knole, Ightham Mote

Clandon Park

West Clandon, Guildford, Surrey GU4 7RQ
Tel: Guildford (01483) 222482

SOIL & TERRAIN: alkaline soil. Level terrain and reasonably sheltered
ALTITUDE: 88.3m (290ft)
GARDENERS: one
SPECIAL FEATURES: modern parterre, 18th-century grotto, Maori meeting hut, herbaceous border, naturalised spring bulbs

Eight-acre garden of generally modern origin surrounding the early 18th-century house by Leoni. The Knyff painting in the house shows the original Dutch-style garden swept away by Capability Brown in 1766 and now represented by a parterre laid out in the 1970s. None of Brown's work is evident in the garden although the landscape beyond, which the NT does not own, contains some traces. The impressive late 18th-century grotto is not thought to be his work. The Maori meeting hut in the grounds, brought back from New Zealand by the 4th Earl of Onslow, is an extremely rare example of its type.

BEST TIMES TO VISIT: In spring for cowslips, magnolia and daffodils
SEASON: April to October
ROUTES: Free wandering around grounds and garden
PLANT SALES: Garden centre (not NT) in park grounds
FACILITIES: Restaurant, WCs, shop in house
FACILITIES FOR DISABLED VISITORS: Ramp to garden. ♿ WC in house
LOCATION: 3m E of Guildford at West Clandon on A247 [186:TQ042512]
OTHER GARDENS IN AREA: Claremont Landscape Garden, Hatchlands, Polesden Lacey, Wisley (not NT)

Claremont Landscape Garden

Portsmouth Road, Esher, Surrey KT10 9JG
Tel: Esher (01372) 469421

SOIL & TERRAIN: light sandy soil. Undulating terrain. S-facing amphitheatre
ALTITUDE: 30m (100ft)
GARDENERS: two full-time; one part-time
SPECIAL FEATURES: fine example of 18th-century landscape garden. Turf amphitheatre probably the most complete in Europe. Camellia terrace

Fifty acres of landscaped garden. One of the most famous gardens in Europe during the 18th century. Conceived by the Duke of Newcastle in 1711 and continued by Lord Clive (Clive of India) in 1768. Landscaping by Vanbrugh, Bridgeman, Kent and Brown between 1711 and 1774. A royal estate in the 19th century. Main area of landscape garden acquired by the NT in 1949 in neglected state. Donations from the Slater Foundation and others enabled garden to be restored between 1975 and 1980. Microcosm of 18th-century English landscape gardening with turf amphitheatre, lake, grotto, island pavilion, bowling green and belvedere tower. Also camellia terrace, dovecote, nine-pin alley and statues of boar and peacock. Delightful walks with ever-changing vistas. Some trees lost in storms of 1987 and 1990.

BEST TIMES TO VISIT: Popular all year. Try to avoid Sundays and Bank Holidays. *Fête champêtre* in mid July
SEASON: All year
PUBLICATIONS: Comprehensive guidebook. Also *The Story of Claremont* by Phylis Cooper
ROUTES: Stone paths meander throughout garden
FACILITIES: Restaurant, shop, WCs, car park
FACILITIES FOR DISABLED VISITORS: Wheelchairs available. Level pathways around lake. Access to amphitheatre viewpoint would require assistance. Guide dogs admitted. Braille guide
LOCATION: On S edge of Esher, on E side of A307 (no access from Esher bypass) [187:TQ128634]
OTHER GARDENS IN AREA: Polesden Lacey, Hatchlands, Clandon, Wisley (not NT), Kew Gardens (not NT), Painshill (not NT), Hampton Court (not NT), Winkworth Arboretum

The Courts

Holt, nr Trowbridge, Wiltshire BA14 6RR
Tel: Trowbridge (01225) 782340

SOIL & TERRAIN: alkaline, heavy soil. Flat terrain and sheltered enclosed garden
ALTITUDE: 60.9m (200ft)
GARDENERS: two
SPECIAL FEATURES: topiary, lily pond, mixed borders and conservatory

Sir George Hastings occupied the house from 1900 to 1911 and planted yew hedges in garden as a background for his collection of stone statuary. In 1920 Major T.C.E. Goff and his wife, Lady

Cecilie, moved to The Courts. Much influenced by the plantings of Gertrude Jekyll and of Lawrence Johnston at Hidcote, and believing a garden should bring surprises at every turn, Lady Cecilie created the 7-acre garden around the basic hedges and statuary left by Sir George Hastings. The result is 3½ acres of formal gardens divided by yew hedges, shrub borders and raised terraces. Features include conservatory, lily pond, mixed borders and pleached limes. A further 3½ acres of arboretum were planted in 1952 with spring bulbs, orchard and hazel coppice.

BEST TIMES TO VISIT: June to July for roses and herbaceous borders
SEASON: April to October
PUBLICATIONS: Leaflet on garden and house
ROUTES: Grass and stone paths for free wandering
FACILITIES FOR DISABLED VISITORS: Limited wheelchair access
LOCATION: 3m SW of Melksham, 2½m E of Bradford-on-Avon on S side of B3107 in centre of Holt [173:ST861618]
OTHER GARDENS IN AREA: Stourhead, Bowood (not NT), Iford Manor (not NT)

Emmetts Garden

Ide Hill, Sevenoaks, Kent TN14 6AY
Tel: Ide Hill (0173 275) 367/429

SOIL & TERRAIN: sandy loam over greensand. Hilltop garden with easterly aspect exposed to S
ALTITUDE: 220m (720ft)
GARDENERS: two full-time; one careership
SPECIAL FEATURES: shrub garden with rare and exotic species. Italianate rose garden and rock garden

Five-acre shrub garden planted towards end of the 19th century, in the informal style of the influential Victorian gardener, William Robinson. Contains exotic species within a natural landscape underplanted with naturalised bulbs. An Italianate rose garden was created in 1910, and the rock garden, which has recently been restored, was built in 1937. The site is one of the highest in Kent, and provides magnificent views of the Weald of Kent and Bough Beech Reservoir.

BEST TIMES TO VISIT: Spring for the flowering shrubs
SEASON: April to end October
PUBLICATIONS: Garden guide
ROUTES: Extensive paths throughout garden
FACILITIES: Tea-room, shop, WCs
FACILITIES FOR DISABLED VISITORS: Good wheelchair access to most of garden. Guide dogs admitted. Scented plants
LOCATION: 1½m S of A25 on Sundridge–Ide Hill road, 1½m N of Ide Hill off B2042 [188:TQ477524]
OTHER GARDENS IN AREA: Chartwell, Knole, Ightham Mote, Quebec House

Ham House

Ham, Richmond, Surrey TW10 7RS Tel: 0181-940 1950

SOIL & TERRAIN: acid, light soil. Flat terrain
ALTITUDE: 15m (45ft)
GARDENERS: three
SPECIAL FEATURES: parterre with box-edged beds filled with lavenders. Arbours, topiary, shrubs, statuary, pavilions in formal wilderness. Orangery believed to be oldest surviving British example

Eighteen-acre 17th-century garden. Restoration begun by the NT in 1970s. Original garden laid out in 1670s principally by the Duke and Duchess of Lauderdale who were also responsible for refurbishing the early 17th-century house. A glimpse of the garden's original glory can be gained from John Evelyn's description in 1678 of: '... the Parterres, Flower Gardens, Orangeries, Groves, Avenues, Courts, Statues, Perspectives, Fountaines, Aviaries, and all this at the banks of the Sweetest River in the World, must needes be surprising.' The hey-day of the garden was brief for by the 18th century it had become neglected. Some formality was lost in the 19th century with the planting of shrubs in the wilderness to disguise the symmetry; gravel paths to the south front were also grassed over. Fortunately very detailed records enabled accurate restoration work. With Westbury Court in Gloucestershire (see p.75), this is one of the oldest surviving garden layouts in Britain.

BEST TIMES TO VISIT: Summer, although good at all times
SEASON: All year
PUBLICATIONS: Guidebook to house and garden
ROUTES: Free wandering throughout garden
FACILITIES: Restaurant, shop, WCs
FACILITIES FOR DISABLED VISITORS: ♿ WC in garden. Wheelchair access but deep gravel paths (ramps to house)
LOCATION: On S bank of Thames, W of A307 at Petersham nr Richmond [176:TQ172732]
OTHER GARDENS IN AREA: Osterley Park, Kew Gardens (not NT), Chiswick House (not NT), Hampton Court (not NT)

Hatchlands Park

East Clandon, Guildford, Surrey GU4 7RT
Tel: Guildford (01483) 222482

SOIL & TERRAIN: acid, heavy soil. Level terrain. Sheltered site
ALTITUDE: 94.4m (300ft)
GARDENERS: two
SPECIAL FEATURES: parterres, statuary, temple, shrubberies and pleasure grounds

Garden surviving in part from 18th century and surrounding brick house built for Admiral Boscawen and set in a park designed by Repton. Garden adapted in Edwardian era by Lord Rendel. Recently restored to incorporate Gertrude Jekyll's design for the south terrace and modification of the west front layout to reflect Repton's influence from surviving evidence. Further restoration of 18th-century features planned for future years.

BEST TIMES TO VISIT: Summer when flower garden at its best
SEASON: April to mid October
PUBLICATIONS: Section in guidebook to property
ROUTES: Paths through park
FACILITIES: Licensed restaurant, WCs, shop
FACILITIES FOR DISABLED VISITORS: Terrace and part of garden accessible to wheelchair users

LOCATION: E of East Clandon, N of A246 Guildford–Leatherhead road [187:TQ063518]
OTHER GARDENS IN AREA: Polesden Lacey, Claremont Landscape Garden, Clandon Park, Wisley (not NT)

Hinton Ampner

Bramdean, nr Alresford, Hampshire SO24 OLA
Tel: Winchester (01962) 771305

SOIL & TERRAIN: alkaline, light soil. Garden on chalk ridge, sloping and terraced. Exposed hilltop site
ALTITUDE: 120m (400ft)
GARDENERS: three

SPECIAL FEATURES: unexpected vistas with eye-catchers and impressive views of surrounding countryside. 600ft-walk flanked by Irish yews. Dell planted with luxuriant foliage plants, including astilbes and hostas in steeply sloping beds. Magnolias and hydrangeas. Orchard

A hilltop garden on chalk ridge of the North Downs some 8 miles east of Winchester. The garden was the creation of Ralph Dutton (later Lord Sherborne) who extended and redesigned the original garden in the 1940s, creating a fine garden on generally rather thin and unpromising soil in an exposed position. The garden combines formal design and informal planting. There are interesting walks and vistas and a good collection of shrubs and plants. Fine views to the south across the parkland to the hills. Suffered greatly from the storms of 1987 and 1990 and many older shrubs and plantings are being replaced in restoration programme. The Hinton Ampner Estate was bequeathed to the NT by the late Lord Sherborne in 1985.

BEST TIMES TO VISIT: Massed planting of daffodils in orchard in spring. Interest through most of summer months
SEASON: April to end September
PUBLICATIONS: Leaflet/plan to garden; also section in property guidebook. Replanting of garden featured in *Story of a Hampshire Manor* by Ralph Dutton (National Trust/Century Classics)

ROUTES: Free wandering
FACILITIES: Tea-room, WCs
FACILITIES FOR DISABLED VISITORS: Wheelchair access to most of garden. ♿WC. Guide dogs admitted
LOCATION: On A272, 1m W of Bramdean village, 8m E of Winchester [185:SU597275]
OTHER GARDENS IN AREA: Mottisfont Abbey, Uppark, The Vyne, Winchester City Mill (tiny island garden)

Ightham Mote

Ivy Hatch, Sevenoaks, Kent TN15 0NT Tel: Plaxtol (01732) 810378

SOIL & TERRAIN: lime-free soil. Level terrain
ALTITUDE: 100m (330ft)
GARDENERS: two; one contract

Beautiful medieval moated manor house set in wooded valley. An extensive lawn has replaced the stewpond which originally supplied the house with fish. The stream which once fed the stewpond now cascades over the grass to fill the moat. Beyond the lawn is an area planted with a mix of native and exotic trees interspersed with paths. Long border near house crammed with traditional English flowers such as sweet Williams, roses and pinks. Paved Fountain Garden to the left of the entrance drive being restored with a lily pool, fountain and pinks and rock roses in the crevices of the paving. Woodland walk and small lake were developed in 1993/94.

BEST TIMES TO VISIT: All season
SEASON: April to end October
PUBLICATIONS: Section in property guidebook
ROUTES: Free wandering throughout garden and woodland
FACILITIES: Tea-bar, shop, WCs, picnic area in car park
FACILITIES FOR DISABLED VISITORS: Wheelchair access to garden. ♿WC
LOCATION: 6m E of Sevenoaks, off A25 [188:TQ584535]
OTHER GARDENS IN AREA: Chartwell, Emmetts, Great Comp (not NT), Hever Castle (not NT), Penshurst Place (not NT)

Lacock Abbey

Lacock, nr Chippenham, Wiltshire SN15 2LG
Tel: Chippenham (01249) 730227

SOIL & TERRAIN: limy. Level terrain
ALTITUDE: 30m (100ft)
GARDENERS: one full-time; one seasonal part-time
SPECIAL FEATURES: early 19th-century rose garden. Diverse range of wild flowers

Thirteenth-century abbey converted to private house in 16th century after Reformation. Set in delightful parkland with cedars and several mature specimen trees including black walnuts, a tulip tree and a swamp cypress. In spring the grass is carpeted with *Crocus vernus*, followed by a fine display of daffodils.

BEST TIMES TO VISIT: Early spring for *Crocus vernus*
SEASON: April to end October. Open for National Gardens Scheme
PUBLICATIONS: Section in property guidebook
ROUTES: Free wandering
FACILITIES: Refreshments available in Lacock village. WCs
FACILITIES FOR DISABLED VISITORS: Grounds accessible to wheelchair users. ♿ WC
LOCATION: 3m S of Chippenham, just E of A350 [173:ST919684]
OTHER GARDENS IN AREA: Bowood (not NT), The Courts

Lamb House

West Street, Rye, East Sussex TN31 7ES Tel: (01892) 890651

SOIL & TERRAIN: medium loam. Garden on hilltop exposed to prevailing SW winds
ALTITUDE: 15m (50ft)
GARDENERS: one part-time

A charming walled garden of approximately an acre in the middle of Rye. At one time laid out by Alfred Parsons. The red-brick walls and house provide a setting for the immaculate lawns and flower beds planted with an interesting collection of garden plants and small shrubs. Home of the writer Henry James from 1898 to 1916.

BEST TIMES TO VISIT: Any time in season
SEASON: April to end October
PUBLICATIONS: Section in guide to property
ROUTES: Good paths throughout garden
FACILITIES: None at property but many shops, tea-rooms in Rye
LOCATION: In West Street, Rye, facing W end of church [198:TQ920202]
OTHER GARDENS IN AREA: Scotney Castle Garden, Great Dixter (not NT)

Mompesson House

The Close, Salisbury, Wiltshire SP1 2EL
Tel: Salisbury (01722) 335659

SOIL & TERRAIN: alkaline, light soil. Walled and sheltered garden with level terrain
ALTITUDE: 20m (70ft)
GARDENERS: one

SPECIAL FEATURES: old roses, blue herbaceous geraniums, *Magnolia grandiflora*, Judas tree, pergola, herbaceous borders, shrubs, ornamental trees

Intimate and sheltered garden enclosed by Cathedral Close wall, house and outbuildings. Today's garden based on design of a central lawn surrounded by paths and herbaceous borders containing wide variety of plants, mostly replanted by the NT since 1975. Features include pergola covered in wisteria, honeysuckle and clematis. Panelled privy set in the Close wall. Lavender walk, paved sitting area and garden room. Scented plants include old roses, *Trachelospermum asiaticum* and, at front of house, *Magnolia grandiflora* and myrtle. Trees include *Magnolia* × *soulangeana* and *Cercis siliquastrum* (Judas tree). Essentially a traditional English garden of great charm.

BEST TIMES TO VISIT: April for flowering of magnolia and Judas tree. Roses and herbaceous borders in summer months. Attractive and peaceful at any time during season
SEASON: April to October
ROUTES: Level and paved paths throughout garden

FACILITIES: Tea-room, WC, garden seats
FACILITIES FOR DISABLED VISITORS: Level garden with few shallow steps. Paved paths. Scented plants such as old roses, honeysuckle, *Trachelospermum asiaticum*
LOCATION: Cathedral Close, centre of Salisbury [184:SU142295]
OTHER GARDENS IN AREA: Mottisfont Abbey, Stourhead

Monk's House

Rodmell, Lewes, East Sussex BN7 3HF Tel: (01892) 890651

SOIL & TERRAIN: alkaline, medium-light soil. Low-lying level ground in Ouse valley
ALTITUDE: 15m (50ft)
GARDENERS: garden maintained by tenant

Monk's House was the home of Leonard and Virginia Woolf from 1919. The garden is still largely as it was in the Woolfs' time. Near the house yew hedges, paths and flintstone walls from an old piggery frame formal herbaceous areas. The orchard leads to the bowling green and dew pond. The garden house where Virginia used to work still contains her writing desk and there is a display of photographs with extracts from her diaries and letters.

BEST TIMES TO VISIT: Spring for bulbs and summer for flowering plants
SEASON: April to October (only open for two afternoons a week)
PUBLICATIONS: Short section in property guidebook
ROUTES: Free wandering throughout garden
FACILITIES: WC
FACILITIES FOR DISABLED VISITORS: Garden not suitable for wheelchair users. Some scented plants and statuary which may be felt. Guide dogs admitted
LOCATION: 4m SE of Lewes in Rodmell village near church [198:TQ421064]
OTHER GARDENS IN AREA: Charleston Farmhouse (not NT), Sheffield Park Garden

Mottisfont Abbey Garden

Mottisfont, nr Romsey, Hampshire
Tel: Lockerley (01794) 341220/340757

SOIL & TERRAIN: alkaline soil. Gently sloping site
ALTITUDE: 45m (150ft)
GARDENERS: three full-time; one part-time

SPECIAL FEATURES: delightful setting by the River Test. Gothick summer house built from parts of the Old Priory. NCCPG National Collection of old roses. Magnificent London plane trees

Twenty-one-acre landscape garden providing the setting for Mottisfont Abbey which was built from the remains of a medieval priory. Superb trees grow in relatively poor soil, but with an ample water supply. Apart from the trees, the garden round the Abbey is mainly early 20th-century and features work by Norah Lindsay and Geoffrey Jellicoe. The Rose Garden, which was laid out by Graham Stuart Thomas in the walled kitchen garden in the 1970s and 1980s, holds the NCCPG National Collection of old roses (pre-1900).

BEST TIMES TO VISIT: June for the rose season (extremely popular at this time). Also very attractive in early spring, May and later in the season

SEASON: April to end October. No special bookings for extended opening in June for rose season

PUBLICATIONS: Described in Abbey guidebook. Also fold out leaflet with bird's-eye plan of the grounds and a separate gazetteer of the Rose Garden. *An English Rose Garden: Gardening with Roses at Mottisfont* by Graham Stuart Thomas (National Trust in association with Michael Joseph)

ROUTES: Free wandering around garden

PLANT SALES: Sales of roses

FACILITIES: Shop, ice-cream kiosk. Refreshments obtainable from Post Office tea-room in village. WCs

FACILITIES FOR DISABLED VISITORS: Rose Garden excellent for visually impaired visitors. Guide dogs admitted. Wheelchair access reasonable but long distances are involved. Motorised buggy available to most parts of garden

LOCATION: 4½m NW of Romsey, ¾m W of A3057 [185:SU327270]
OTHER GARDENS IN AREA: Exbury (not NT), Hillier Arboretum at Braishfield (not NT), Hinton Ampner

Nymans Garden

Handcross, nr Haywards Heath, West Sussex RH17 6EB
Tel: Handcross (01444) 400321/400002

SOIL & TERRAIN: acid, light soil. Undulating terrain on exposed hilltop
ALTITUDE: 152m (500ft)
GARDENERS: six

Thirty-acre garden on the Sussex Weald famous for its rare collection of plants. Created by the Messel family over three generations from 1890. Originally planned around a pastiche '14th-century' manor house which was gutted by fire in 1947 and now forms a picturesque shell. Intention to display as wide a variety of plants as possible from all over the world. Particular features include the collection of magnolias, rhododendrons and other flowering tree and shrubs. In high summer the double flower borders are a striking feature. Pinetum recently replanted after devastation of the 1987 storm which destroyed many fine specimens. Plants hybridised at Nymans include *Camellia* 'Leonard Messel'. Hidden sunken garden.

BEST TIMES TO VISIT: Spring for carpets of daffodils. Summer for roses and colourful herbaceous borders. Autumn colour spectacular with Japanese maples
SEASON: April to end October
PUBLICATIONS: Guide to garden. Leaflets on seasonal walks
ROUTES: Paths throughout garden
PLANT SALES: Large variety of plants available
FACILITIES: Tea-room, WCs, shop
FACILITIES FOR DISABLED VISITORS: Good wheelchair access on the level from car park to most areas of the garden (route indicated). Some aromatic plants
LOCATION: 4½m S of Crawley off M23/A23 [187:TQ265294]
OTHER GARDENS IN AREA: Wakehurst Place, Sheffield Park Garden, Leonardslee Gardens (not NT), Borde Hill (not NT)

Petworth House

Petworth, West Sussex GU28 0AE Tel: Petworth (01793) 342207

SOIL & TERRAIN: acid mixed soil. Undulating terrain, exposed site
ALTITUDE: 60.9m (200ft)
GARDENERS: four

SPECIAL FEATURES: massive ancient trees, lakes, temples, good views to north and south. 1,000 fallow deer. Water fowl

The grounds surrounding the magnificent 17th-century house consist of two distinct areas: the deer park and the pleasure grounds. The 650-acre ancient deer park includes two lakes and undulating tree-capped hills and is home to a herd of 1,000 fallow deer. Near to the house in 1752 Capability Brown rounded, smoothed and replanted George London's late 17th-century formal terraces and created the lakes by damming and ducting local underground springs. Since the storms of 1987 and 1990 35,000 trees have been planted. Before the 1987 storm nine of the tallest trees in the country stood in the pleasure grounds, which were devastated by the storm. They have now been largely replanted. Both formal and informal influences have been incorporated into its new design with herbaceous borders, bulbs and wild flowers.

BEST TIMES TO VISIT: Pleasure grounds: April to June for bulbs and wild flowers; June to August for herbaceous borders; October for autumn colour. Park: attractive throughout year
SEASON: Pleasure grounds: April to end October. Park: all year
PUBLICATIONS: Sections on grounds and garden in property guidebook (pre-storm). Park leaflet
ROUTES: Free wandering in parkland. Surfaced paths in pleasure grounds. Information board in car park shows routes
FACILITIES: Restaurant, tea-room, WCs, shop (when house open)
FACILITIES FOR DISABLED VISITORS: Wheelchair access, guide dogs admitted. ♿ WC in servants' block at house when house open (April to end October)
LOCATION: At Petworth on A272 [197:SU976218]
OTHER GARDENS IN AREA: Winkworth Arboretum, Nymans Garden, Uppark, Oakhurst Cottage (by appointment only)

Polesden Lacey

nr Dorking, Surrey RH5 6BD
Tel: Bookham (01372) 458203/452048

SOIL & TERRAIN: alkaline, light soil. Garden has a gentle N–S slope. Exposed hilltop site on North Downs
ALTITUDE: 91m (300ft)
GARDENERS: five

SPECIAL FEATURES: walled Edwardian-style gardens. Sweeping lawns with mature trees. Rose Garden and fine herbaceous border

The Polesden Lacey Estate was left to the NT by the Honourable Mrs Ronald Greville, a renowned society hostess, in 1942. The gardens, which were Mrs Greville's creation, follow an Edwardian theme. Walled Rose Garden (outside which Mrs Greville is buried) and separate lavender, iris and peony gardens. There are fine views from the lawns and from the Long Walk (started in 1761, predating most of the garden) to the surrounding countryside. Notable herbaceous border and a winter garden. Some interesting statues and garden ornaments many of which were collected by Mrs Greville.

BEST TIMES TO VISIT: June to July for the Rose Garden. If possible avoid weekends and Bank Holidays
SEASON: All year
PUBLICATIONS: Garden guide and leaflet
ROUTES: Free wandering. Paths in formal gardens
FACILITIES: Restaurant/tea-room, WCs, shop
FACILITIES FOR DISABLED VISITORS: Wheelchair access to parts of garden. Guide dogs admitted. Rose and lavender gardens scented
LOCATION: 5m NW of Dorking, 2m S of Great Bookham, off A246 Leatherhead–Guildford road [187:TQ136522]
OTHER GARDENS IN AREA: Winkworth Arboretum, Claremont Landscape Garden, Clandon Park, Hatchlands, Wisley (not NT), Painshill Park (not NT)

Scotney Castle Garden

Lamberhurst, Tunbridge Wells, Kent TN3 8JN
Tel: Lamberhurst (01892) 890651

SOIL & TERRAIN: lime-free. Steep site
ALTITUDE: 75m (250ft)
GARDENERS: four full-time; one occasional part-time

SPECIAL FEATURES: romantic landscape garden. Circular herb garden by Lanning Roper

A romantic, picturesque landscape garden primarily conceived by William Sawrey Gilpin between 1833 and 1843, when the new mansion was being built for Edward Hussey by the architect Anthony Salvin (1799–1881). Parts of the old 14th-century castle were taken down in such a way as to retain features of interest, and increase the romantic character of the scene, surrounded as it is by the moat. There are many dramatic vistas due to the steep lie of the land, which is planted with trees and flowering shrubs for all-year colour, with a delicate balance between deciduous and evergreen plants. On a small isthmus stands a bronze by Henry Moore. Another interesting feature is the 18th-century ice house.

BEST TIMES TO VISIT: Spring for shrubs in bloom
SEASON: April to end October
PUBLICATIONS: Guidebook to garden. *Lanning Roper* by Jane Brown
ROUTES: Extensive paths throughout garden
FACILITIES: WCs, shop
FACILITIES FOR DISABLED VISITORS: Wheelchair access (strong pusher needed in some cases). Guide dogs admitted
LOCATION: 1m S of Lamberhurst on A21 [188:TQ688353]
OTHER GARDENS IN AREA: Chartwell, Emmetts Garden, Bedgebury Pinetum (not NT), Sprivers Garden

Sheffield Park Garden

Uckfield, East Sussex TN22 3QX Tel: Danehill (01825) 790231

SOIL & TERRAIN: lime-free soil. Sloping site
ALTITUDE: 91m (300ft)
GARDENERS: five
SPECIAL FEATURES: wide collection of rare trees and shrubs

One-hundred-acre garden with ornamental lakes originally laid out by Capability Brown for the Earl of Sheffield in 1776 but transformed by Arthur Soames after he acquired the estate in 1909. Soames was responsible for introducing the exciting collection of rare and unusual trees and shrubs and provided an inspired planting scheme giving colour throughout the year. In spring wild flowers and bulbs, woodland glades and rhododendrons, azaleas, kalmias and other flowering shrubs provide exciting banks of colour. Late-flowering rhododendrons follow in summer with water-lilies and gunnera. Autumn is spectacular at Sheffield Park with maples, fothergillas, Spanish chestnuts and tupelo trees and many other deciduous trees providing breath-taking colour against a backdrop of evergreen cypresses, cedars and pines, while Chinese *Gentiana sino-ornata* and autumn crocuses flower at ground level. Stream garden with good display of irises and astilbes. At all seasons the foliage and vegetation is beautifully reflected in the lakes adding another dimension to this stunning garden.

BEST TIMES TO VISIT: Something of interest at all times
SEASON: April to November
PUBLICATIONS: Guidebook to garden
ROUTES: Garden and woodland criss-crossed by gravel and grass paths
FACILITIES: Shop, WCs, car park, picnic area
FACILITIES FOR DISABLED VISITORS: Garden accessible for wheelchairs. Wheelchairs and motorised buggy available. Guide dogs admitted. Textured tree bark. ♿WC
LOCATION: Midway between East Grinstead and Lewes, 5m NW of Uckfield on E side of A275 [198:TQ415240]
OTHER GARDENS IN AREA: Standen, Wakehurst Place Garden, Borde Hill Garden (not NT), Leonardslee Gardens (not NT), Nymans Garden

Sissinghurst Garden

Sissinghurst, nr Cranbrook, Kent TN17 2AB
Tel: Cranbrook (01580) 712850 (visitor information) or 715330 (party bookings)

SOIL & TERRAIN: mainly lime-free soil. Level terrain
ALTITUDE: 60.9m (200ft)
GARDENERS: six

SPECIAL FEATURES: variety of colour and design within series of outdoor rooms

The magical garden of Sissinghurst is the creation of Vita Sackville-West and Sir Harold Nicolson who moved here in 1930 and transformed the collection of run-down ancient buildings and the surrounding garden. The garden was divided into a series of compartments and each 'room' was filled with an inspired and informal arrangement of plants around a certain theme: these include the White Garden, the Purple Border, the Rose Garden, the Herb Garden, the Lime Walk and the Cottage Garden. The White Garden shows Vita Sackville-West's feeling for colour at its height. *Rosa longicuspis* erupts into a cascade of white flowers in summer, surrounded by numerous other plants with grey foliage and white blossoms. Other areas show the same ingenuity of planting.

BEST TIMES TO VISIT: Throughout season. Always something of interest. Timed ticket system in operation and the daily visitor numbers are restricted. The garden may be closed at short notice once its daily capacity is reached
SEASON: April to October
PUBLICATIONS: Garden guidebook. *Sissinghurst* by Anne Scott-James, *Vita's Other World* by Jane Brown, *Sissinghurst* by Jane Brown (National Trust/Weidenfeld and Nicolson)
ROUTES: Narrow paths throughout garden
PLANT SALES: Surplus plants propagated for the garden occasionally available
FACILITIES: Restaurant, shop, picnic area, WCs, exhibition
FACILITIES FOR DISABLED VISITORS: Wheelchair access restricted to two chairs at any one time because of narrow and uneven paths. Plan of recommended wheelchair route available. Guide dogs admitted. Scented plants

LOCATION: 2m NE of Cranbrook, 1m E of Sissinghurst village (A262) [188:TQ8138]
OTHER GARDENS IN AREA: Bedgebury Pinetum (not NT), Scotney Castle Garden, Great Dixter (not NT)

Standen

East Grinstead, West Sussex RH19 4NE
Tel: East Grinstead (01342) 323029

SOIL & TERRAIN: fertile, sandy soil. S-facing site, steeply sloping terrain
ALTITUDE: 60.9m (200ft)
GARDENERS: one full-time; one part-time
SPECIAL FEATURES: good aspect and views. Quarry garden with ferns. Catmint

Family house designed by Philip Webb, friend of William Morris, in 1890s. Charming 12-acre garden on several levels linked by flights of steps with magnificent views across valley. Upper areas of garden planted with acers, azaleas and rhododendrons. Fine example of tulip tree and good ground cover throughout garden. Rose garden planted with varieties of Rugosa.

BEST TIMES TO VISIT: Late spring, early summer and autumn for rhododendrons, azaleas and woodland flowers
SEASON: April to end October
PUBLICATIONS: Section in property guidebook
ROUTES: Free wandering throughout garden. Also woodland walks
FACILITIES: Tea-room, shop, WCs
FACILITIES FOR DISABLED VISITORS: Garden partly accessible to wheelchair users but steps and gravel paths
LOCATION: 2m S of East Grinstead, signposted from B2110 [187:TQ389356]
OTHER GARDENS IN AREA: Wakehurst Place Garden, Nymans Garden, Sheffield Park Garden

Stourhead

Stourton, Warminster, Wiltshire BA12 6QH
Tel: Bourton (01747) 841152

SOIL & TERRAIN: lime-free soil. Sloping terrain leading down to lake
ALTITUDE: 152m (500ft)
GARDENERS: six
SPECIAL FEATURES: 18th-century landscape layout. Exotic trees

Magnificent landscape garden created by Henry Hoare II, the wealthy banker, from 1741–80 as a reaction against formal gardens of the 17th century. 'Natural' landscape dotted with classical eye-catchers surrounds a long artificial lake and presents an English 18th-century view of an arcadian paradise. Follies include a Pantheon, Temple of Apollo, Temple of Flora and a dripping grotto with a river god. Richard Colt Hoare, grandson of Henry, added to the garden by planting unusual trees and shrubs but left his grandfather's basic scheme unaltered. Daffodils carpet the grounds in spring when magnolias are in flower and a stunning display of rhododendrons follows in early summer. Japanese and Norwegian bloodleaf maples, tulip trees and other exotics give a blazing autumn display.

BEST TIMES TO VISIT: Something of interest all year: spring flowers and shrubs, rhododendrons May to June and autumn colour. *Fête champêtre* in July
SEASON: All year
PUBLICATIONS: Colour souvenir guide. Tree list. *The Stourhead Landscape* and *Landscape and Antiquity: Aspects of English Culture at Stourhead 1718 to 1838* by Kenneth Woodbridge
ROUTES: Paths lead throughout the garden
FACILITIES: Visitor Centre, WCs, parents' room, shop. Refreshments at Spread Eagle Inn and Village Hall Restaurant in yard.
FACILITIES FOR DISABLED VISITORS: Route around lake suitable for wheelchair users with a strong pusher. Motorised buggy available. ♿ WC at Visitor Centre and Spread Eagle. Guide dogs admitted. Scented azaleas, Philadelphus
LOCATION: At Stourton off B3092, 3m NW of Mere [183:ST7834]
OTHER GARDENS IN AREA: The Courts, Hadspen House (not NT), Iford Manor (not NT)

The Vyne

Sherborne St John, Basingstoke, Hampshire RG26 5DX
Tel: Basingstoke (01256) 881337

SOIL & TERRAIN: neutral heavy clay. Almost level terrain. Frost pocket
ALTITUDE: 60.9m (200ft)
GARDENERS: one

SPECIAL FEATURES: herbaceous border, lawns, lake, wild garden. Good specimens of *Phillyrea latifolia*. 17th-century garden house

Twelve-acre pleasure grounds in a delightful rural setting surrounding the 16th-century house. The original 18th-century parkland was much reduced between 1840 and 1879 by William Wigget Chute. The area surrounding the house was levelled and sweeping lawns were created. An ornamental lake is the main feature in the grounds. The herbaceous border planted by Major-General Estcourt in 1960 has some unusual perennials and when in full flower (July) provides a marvellous show.

BEST TIMES TO VISIT: July for herbaceous border
SEASON: April to end October
PUBLICATIONS: Section in property guidebook
ROUTES: Free wandering around the gardens
FACILITIES: Tea-room, WCs, shop
FACILITIES FOR DISABLED VISITORS: Reasonable wheelchair access to grounds. ♿ WC
LOCATION: 4m N of Basingstoke between Bramley and Sherborne St John [175 & 186:SU637566]
OTHER GARDENS IN AREA: Basildon Park, Hinton Ampner

Wakehurst Place Garden

Ardingly, Haywards Heath, West Sussex RH17 6TN
Tel: Ardingly (01444) 892701

SOIL & TERRAIN: acid, heavy soil, clay with some sandstone outcrops. Undulating with some small steep valleys
ALTITUDE: 60.9–136m (200–450ft)
GARDENERS: staffed by Royal Botanic Gardens, Kew. Scientific and research work also undertaken at property
SPECIAL FEATURES: rhododendrons. Superb collection of exotic trees, shrubs and plants: several specialist groups including birches, southern beech, hypericums and skimmias. Native trees alternate with exotics such as redwoods, Japanese cedars, Douglas firs and hickories

The mansion and gardens at Wakehurst Place are owned by the NT but leased to the Royal Botanic Gardens, Kew, who administer, fund and maintain the property. Primarily the creation of Gerald Loder, later Lord Wakehurst, who bought the estate in 1903. The gardens are used to display those plants which do not thrive at Kew because of soil and climatic conditions. Superb collection of plants and shrubs arranged according to geographical location. Extensive water, winter and walled gardens featuring many rare and interesting plants from all parts of the world.

BEST TIMES TO VISIT: Spring for bluebells and wild flowers in woodland. May for rhododendrons. June to September for water and walled gardens. Autumn for colour
SEASON: All year
PUBLICATIONS: Guide to garden. Trails and information sheets
ROUTES: Good paths throughout
FACILITIES: Restaurant, shop, guide service, WCs
FACILITIES FOR DISABLED VISITORS: Most of upper garden accessible to wheelchairs. [wheelchair symbol] WC. Guide dogs admitted
LOCATION: 1½m NW of Ardingly on B2028 [187:TQ339314]
OTHER GARDENS IN AREA: Nymans Garden, Sheffield Park Garden, Standen, Petworth

Winkworth Arboretum

Hascombe Road, Munstead, Godalming, Surrey GU8 4AD
Tel: Guildford (01483) 208477

SOIL & TERRAIN: acid, light soil. Hillside site exposed to winds with some isolated frost pockets
ALTITUDE: 60.9m (200ft)
GARDENERS: three

SPECIAL FEATURES: NCCPG National Collection of *Sorbus* Section Aria and Micromeles. Many rare trees and shrubs: *Acer*, *Sorbus*, magnolias, *Ilex*, *Betula*, *Prunus*, rhododendrons and azaleas

Winkworth Arboretum was created by Dr Wilfrid Fox just before the Second World War and the bulk of it was given to the NT in 1952. The collection of rare trees and shrubs is on a steep hillside sloping down to two lakes with fine views to the countryside beyond. The Arboretum holds the National Collection of *Sorbus* Section Aria, and there are many fine rhododendrons and azaleas giving early spring colour together with bluebells and other spring bulbs. A wide variety of trees gives extremely good autumn colour.

BEST TIMES TO VISIT: Spring for bluebells and azaleas. Autumn for colour. Can become rather crowded at weekends and Bank Holidays
SEASON: All year daily during daylight hours
PUBLICATIONS: Guidebook and plan
ROUTES: Free wandering on paths. Dogs to be kept on lead
FACILITIES: Tea-room, WCs, shop
FACILITIES FOR DISABLED VISITORS: Limited wheelchair access, viewpoint and lake are accessible from lower entrance. Guide dogs admitted. Textured tree bark
LOCATION: Near Hascombe, 2m SE of Godalming on E side of B2130 [169, 170 & 186:SU990412]
OTHER GARDENS IN AREA: Polesden Lacey, Claremont Landscape Garden, Clandon Park, Hatchlands Park

Wales and the Welsh Borders

WALES · AVON · GLOUCESTERSHIRE
HEREFORD & WORCESTER · SHROPSHIRE

Attingham Park

Shrewsbury, Shropshire SY4 4TP Tel: (01743) 709203

SOIL & TERRAIN: light soil. Flat, sheltered terrain
ALTITUDE: 30m (100ft)
GARDENERS: two

SPECIAL FEATURES: Repton landscape. Rhododendron walk

The famous landscape gardener Humphry Repton was commissioned to 'improve' the landscape and create a setting worthy of the vast mansion house at Attingham. The NT's management of the property refers closely to these proposals as laid out in Repton's 'Red Book' for Attingham. The pleasant 'Mile Walk' takes the visitor along the River Tern past a variety of trees and shrubs. Recent plantings have taken into account historical lists of shrubs prepared by Leggatt (1770). The path continues past the orchard, gardeners' cottages (now housing a landscape exhibition) and walled garden. Another walk takes visitors through the Deer Park and Attingham woods, past Lord Berwick's memorial.

BEST TIMES TO VISIT: Early spring for daffodils. Late spring for rhododendrons. All-year round for landscape and river walk
SEASON: All year
PUBLICATIONS: Guidebook and park leaflet
ROUTES: Various paths around grounds and Deer Park (Deer Park walk is waymarked)
FACILITIES: Restaurant, shop (April to October). WC all year
FACILITIES FOR DISABLED VISITORS: Wheelchair access. ♿WC
LOCATION: 4m SE of Shrewsbury, on N side of the Telford road on B4380 (formerly A5) at Atcham [126:SJ550099]
OTHER GARDENS IN AREA: Hodnet Hall Garden (not NT), Benthall Hall, Dudmaston, Powis Castle

Benthall Hall

Broseley, Shropshire TF12 5RX Tel: Telford (01952) 882159

SOIL & TERRAIN: alkaline, heavy soil. Exposed site on hilltop with woodland
ALTITUDE: 189m (620ft)
GARDENERS: the two tenants; one full-time horticultural student
SPECIAL FEATURES: George Maw's naturalised crocuses, spring bulbs and unusual plants

Garden of small Elizabethan manor house built by the Benthall family who moved away in the 18th century but repurchased the property in 1934. Home of George Maw and his plant collections 1860–90, some plants now naturalised in the grounds. Subsequently the home of Robert Bateman, son of James Bateman of Biddulph Grange, who was responsible for some of the present garden. Acquired by the NT in 1960. Replanted under the guidance of Graham Stuart Thomas. The Benthall family have continued to occupy the house as tenants and have done much, with the support of the NT, to maintain the interest and peaceful beauty of this small plantsman's garden.

BEST TIMES TO VISIT: Spring for bulbs and early flowering trees. Early summer for roses. Busy on Bank Holiday Mondays
SEASON: April to end September
PUBLICATIONS: Plantlist with plan
ROUTES: Free wandering within limits marked by 'Private' signs
FACILITIES: WC
FACILITIES FOR DISABLED VISITORS: Limited wheelchair access. Guide dogs admitted. Many scented plants
LOCATION: 1m NW of Broseley (B4375), 4m NE of Much Wenlock, 2m S of Ironbridge [127:SJ658025]
OTHER GARDENS IN AREA: Dudmaston, Moseley Old Hall, Hodnet Hall (not NT)

Berrington Hall

nr Leominster, Hereford & Worcester HR6 0DW
Tel: Leominster (01568) 615721

SOIL & TERRAIN: heavy, neutral soil. Sheltered aspect

ALTITUDE: 106m (350ft)
GARDENERS: two

Henry Holland's Berrington Hall with huge temple portico commands large-scale, unspoilt park by Capability Brown, begun in 1775 for Rt. Hon. Thomas Harley. Berrington Pool with wooded island is centrepiece of original scheme. Edwardian formal layout between house and Archway Lodge by Dobies of Chester survives in outline only: rows of clipped golden yew, fountain pool and south-facing wall now with interesting subjects – *Abutilon* and *Buddleja colvilei*. 1930s woodland garden with rhododendron species north of house. 18th-century walled garden recently planted with historic apple varieties. Ha-ha.

BEST TIMES TO VISIT: May for display of rhododendrons. Garden does not get crowded
PUBLICATIONS: Section in property guidebook
ROUTES: Free wandering, limited access to parkland during normal opening hours, July to September. Walled garden scheme at present under development
FACILITIES: WCs, shop, licensed restaurant
FACILITIES FOR DISABLED VISITORS: Wheelchair access. Wheelchair available. Guide dogs admitted. Scented plants
LOCATION: 3m N of Leominster on W side of A49 [137:SO510637]
OTHER GARDENS IN AREA: Croft Castle, The Weir, Hergest Croft Garden (not NT), Burford House Garden (not NT), Brobury Garden (not NT)

Bodnant Garden

Tal-y-Cafn, Colwyn Bay, Clwyd LL28 5RE
Tel: Tyn-y-Groes (01492) 650460

SOIL & TERRAIN: acid, heavy soil overlying boulder clay and shale rock. Garden is steep in places. Site reasonably sheltered
ALTITUDE: 30m (100ft)
GARDENERS: eighteen
SPECIAL FEATURES: NCCPG National Collections of *Embothrium, Eucryphia, Magnolia, Rhododendron forrestii* agg.

Situated on a beautiful site above the River Conwy looking towards Snowdonia, the 80 acres of Bodnant Garden are crammed with variety. Vast collection of plants from all parts of the world. Fine conifers and deciduous trees, large collection of magnolias, camellias and rhododendrons, many of which were raised at Bodnant, such as *Rhododendrons* Fabia, Matador, Vanessa and Winsome. Garden contains yew hedges, formal lily ponds, a natural dell garden, herbaceous borders and extensive terraces. Also a marvellous laburnum arch – a blaze of yellow in early summer.

BEST TIMES TO VISIT: March for daffodils and early magnolias. April for camellias and rhododendrons. May for rhododendrons, azaleas and laburnum arch. June to August for terraced gardens, roses, herbaceous border and water-lilies. Oct for autumn colour
SEASON: Mid March to end October
PUBLICATIONS: Full-colour garden guidebook with plan
ROUTES: Network of paths throughout garden. Recommended routes described in property guidebook
PLANT SALES: Trees and shrubs propagated in the nursery on sale throughout year
FACILITIES: Refreshment pavilion, WCs
FACILITIES FOR DISABLED VISITORS: Garden very steep in places but route avoiding these areas and suitable for wheelchairs is marked in guidebook. Guide dogs admitted. Braille guidebook. Scented plants and textured tree bark throughout garden
LOCATION: 8m S of Llandudno off A470 [115 & 116:SH801723]
OTHER GARDENS IN AREA: Penrhyn Castle

Chirk Castle

Chirk, Clwyd LL14 5AF Tel: Chirk (01691) 777701

SOIL & TERRAIN: very light, well-drained sandy loam, barely inches deep in parts of the garden. Gentle slope on top of a hill. Site exposed to W and E

ALTITUDE: 213m (700ft)

GARDENERS: three permanent; one trainee

A 5½-acre family garden, parts of which date back to the 17th century. The yews in the formal garden were planted after 1872 by Richard Myddelton Biddulph. Rose garden contains mainly floribunda roses and was probably created at the turn of the century. The long shrub border was a herbaceous border in the 1920s but is now a mixed border for easier maintenance. The shrub garden features many fine plants, a huge larch reputed to be 300 years old, many magnolias, hydrangeas, rhododendrons. Fine views over Shropshire and Cheshire from the terrace. A classical garden pavilion designed by William Emes stands at the end of the terrace. A lime tree avenue underplanted with daffodils leads from the terrace up to an early 18th-century statue of Hercules. The rockery contains an abundance of plants and flowers all through the year. Below the rockery is the hawk house built in the early 1900s and now home to fan-tailed doves. Lord Howard de Walden kept 8 hawks here which were tethered in niches in the large yew hedges on the terrace. Many old roses, climbing plants on walls of castle. Embothriums.

BEST TIMES TO VISIT: April to May for rhododendrons, daffodils, magnolias. Many roses in July. Rockery interesting throughout year. Quite busy in July and August but never too crowded

SEASON: April to end October

PUBLICATIONS: Garden leaflet includes a plan and descriptions of numbered areas in garden. Also section in main guidebook

ROUTES: Gravel and grass paths. Free wandering in some areas

FACILITIES: Restaurant, tea-room, WCs, shop

FACILITIES FOR DISABLED VISITORS: Wheelchair access quite good. Guide dogs admitted. Many scented plants. ♿WC

LOCATION: 12m SE of Wrexham, 6m NW of Oswestry on Welsh border, $\frac{1}{2}$m W of Chirk village off A5, 1$\frac{1}{2}$m of private driveway to Castle [117:SJ269381]
OTHER GARDENS IN AREA: Powis Castle, Erddig

Clevedon Court

Clevedon, Avon BS21 6QU Tel: Clevedon (01275) 872257

SOIL & TERRAIN: limy soil. Steeply sloping site
ALTITUDE: 30m (100ft)
GARDENERS: one

Garden of 14th-century Clevedon Court rises behind the house, on two terraces. Originally these south-facing terraces had espaliered fruit trees but are now planted with tender species such as the Judas tree, strawberry tree, *Canna iridiflora*, palms, myrtle, fuchsias and wonderful magnolias. A Gothick summerhouse on one of the terraces counterbalances an 18th-century garden house on the other. Wooded area of ilex above the terraces.

BEST TIMES TO VISIT: Spring for magnolias and Judas tree
SEASON: April to end September
PUBLICATIONS: Section in property guidebook
ROUTES: Free wandering on paths throughout garden
FACILITIES: WC, tea-room
FACILITIES FOR DISABLED VISITORS: Not recommended to wheelchair users because of steep site
LOCATION: 1$\frac{1}{2}$m E of Clevedon on Bristol road (B3130) [172:ST423716]
OTHER GARDENS IN AREA: Dyrham Park

Colby Woodland Garden

Colby Lodge Bothy, Amroth, Narberth, Dyfed SA67 8PP
Tel: Amroth (01834) 811725

SOIL & TERRAIN: lime-free soil. Narrow wooded valley, sheltered from N but vulnerable to E winds

ALTITUDE: 100m (330ft)
GARDENERS: one full-time; one seasonal

Twenty-four acres of informal landscape featuring a small walled garden with a 'gothic gazebo' and 8 acres of woodland garden. The woodland garden, originally set out at the beginning of this century, was left to the NT in 1979. After severe storm damage in 1984 a large part of the woodland garden was replanted with some 400 rhododendrons and associated plants. Planting continues.

BEST TIMES TO VISIT: April to the end of June for the rhododendrons and the woodland garden
SEASON: April to end October
PUBLICATIONS: Leaflet
ROUTES: Free wandering, paths marked in leaflet. Also several miles of waymarked footpath around Colby Estate
PLANT SALES: Specialist plant sales: woodland, rock, herbs, baskets and terracotta pots
FACILITIES: Tea-room, shop, WCs, picnic area, gallery
FACILITIES FOR DISABLED VISITORS: ♿ WCs. Parts of garden accessible to wheelchair users. Prior arrangement appreciated
LOCATION: 1m inland from Amroth in Pembrokeshire. Leave A477, St Clears–Pembroke road at Llanteg [158:SN155080]
OTHER GARDENS IN AREA: Upton Park (not NT), Picton Castle (not NT)

Croft Castle

nr Leominster, Hereford & Worcester HR6 9PW
Tel: Yarpole (01568) 85246

SOIL & TERRAIN: light soil. Exposed parkland site

ALTITUDE: 167m (550ft)
GARDENERS: one

A great park on south-facing slope with 17th-century formal avenues. Traces of 17th-century terraces south of castle. Large area within late 18th-century ha-ha is grazed or mown. Access via 'Picturesque' Gothick gateway near which, in season, is a spectacular drift of cyclamen. Fishpool Valley is an important example of the dramatic Picturesque landscape manner, the chief proponent of which, Richard Payne Knight, lived nearby. Walled garden from 18th and 19th centuries has modern vineyard and herbaceous planting.

BEST TIMES TO VISIT: Autumn for cyclamen. July to August for herbaceous colour
SEASON: April to end October
PUBLICATIONS: Section in property guidebook
ROUTES: Free wandering
FACILITIES: WCs in house. Tea-room and shop at nearby Berrington Hall
FACILITIES FOR DISABLED VISITORS: Wheelchair access. Guide dogs admitted
LOCATION: 5m NW of Leominster, 9m SW of Ludlow [137:SO455655]
OTHER GARDENS IN AREA: Berrington Hall, The Weir, Hergest Croft Garden (not NT), Burford House Gardens (not NT)

Dudmaston

Quatt, nr Bridgnorth, Shropshire WV15 6QN
Tel: Quatt (01746) 780866

SOIL & TERRAIN: acid, light soil. Sloping site. Frost pocket
ALTITUDE: 75m (250ft)
GARDENERS: one full-time; one part-time

Eight-acre garden sloping to lake, with many fine trees and shrubs, particularly rhododendrons and azaleas. Dingle Walk along lake and through wooded valley with stream and large trees.

BEST TIMES TO VISIT: April to June for rhododendrons and azaleas
SEASON: April to end October
PUBLICATIONS: Section in property guidebook

ROUTES: Free wandering
PLANT SALES: Plant sales when house is open
FACILITIES: Tea-room, WCs, shop, car park, picnic area
FACILITIES FOR DISABLED VISITORS: Wheelchair access. Guide dogs admitted. Some scented plants (azaleas)
LOCATION: 4m SE of Bridgnorth on A442 [138:SO746887]
OTHER GARDENS IN AREA: Wightwick Manor, Swallow Hayes (not NT), Gatacre Park (not NT), Preen Manor (not NT)

Dyrham Park

Dyrham, nr Chippenham, Avon SN14 8ER
Tel: Abson (01272) 372501

SOIL & TERRAIN: limy soil. Deer park on steep slope. Garden relatively level
ALTITUDE: 136m (450ft)
GARDENERS: one full-time; one part-time seasonal

Little remains of the magnificent 17th-century water garden at Dyrham Park captured by Kip in his view of 1712. Now Dyrham's grounds are largely taken up by parkland planned by Charles Harcourt-Master in the 18th century with fine trees including beeches, chestnuts and cedars. A herd of fallow deer roams the parkland. The garden to the rear of the house includes flower and shrub beds and a large pond.

BEST TIMES TO VISIT: Something of interest all season
SEASON: Garden: April to end October. Park: all year
PUBLICATIONS: Section in property guidebook
ROUTES: Free wandering throughout garden and parkland
FACILITIES: Tea-room, WC
FACILITIES FOR DISABLED VISITORS: Not recommended to wheelchair users as park is on a steep gradient and garden only accessible via a series of steps from the terrace (access through house)
LOCATION: 8m N of Bath, 12m E of Bristol on A46 [172:ST743757]
OTHER GARDENS IN AREA: Bristol Botanic Garden (not NT), Claverton Manor (not NT), Westonbirt Arboretum (not NT), Westbury Court Garden

Erddig

nr Wrexham, Clwyd LL13 0YT Tel: Wrexham (01978) 355314

SOIL & TERRAIN: borderline neutral soil. Acid-loving plants can be grown. Level terrain. Exposed to E. Walls can cause frost pockets
ALTITUDE: 60.9m (200ft)
GARDENERS: four
SPECIAL FEATURES: NCCPG National Collection of ivy, old fruit varieties, canal, naturalised bulbs, herb bed

18th-century garden attached to house within wooded and landscaped park. Restored by the NT from historical archive evidence. Formal garden divided into lawns. Many old varieties of espaliered and fan-trained fruit trees, wall shrubs and climbers underplanted with old varieties of daffodils, narcissi and herbaceous plants. Central walk lined with 'mock' orange tree boxes of Portuguese laurels and bordered by 'pleached' lime trees leads to central canal and 18th-century gates. Victorian bedded parterre and gardens with shrub and climbing roses.

BEST TIMES TO VISIT: Always something of interest from spring bulbs through to fruit in autumn
SEASON: April to mid October
PUBLICATIONS: Section in property guidebook. Garden guide. Plan of route around property and walks through woods and estate
ROUTES: Free access at all times in park. Free wandering in garden. Garden tours and other events available
PLANT SALES: Small plant sales outlet planned
FACILITIES: Restaurant, tea-room, WCs, shop
FACILITIES FOR DISABLED VISITORS: Wheelchair access to most areas of garden (forward notice of visit should be given for those requiring loan of wheelchair as only one available). Herb border/scented plants. Guide dogs admitted
LOCATION: 2m S of Wrexham, signposted A525 Whitchurch road, or A483/A5152 [117:SJ326482]
OTHER GARDENS IN AREA: Chirk Castle, Powis Castle, Tatton Park, Dunham Massey

Hanbury Hall

Droitwich, Hereford & Worcester WR9 7EA
Tel: Hanbury (01527) 821214

SOIL & TERRAIN: neutral clay. Level site

ALTITUDE: 60.9m (200ft)
GARDENERS: one

Work began in the autumn of 1993 to recreate a garden of *c.*1700 designed by George London, the leading practitioner of his day. To date three principal elements have been recreated: the Sunken Parterre, Wilderness and Fruit Garden. George London's garden relied on dividing the area up into contrasting compartments with a liberal sprinkling of summerhouses. The lawn within the ha-ha sweeps round to reveal a fine orangery *c.*1740 with orange trees. An original cedar from the London design remains together with a replanted avenue leading to a well-preserved 18th-century ice house. The forecourt, formerly severe and stately with gravel, grass and ironwork, now contains modern borders.

BEST TIMES TO VISIT: Spring and summer
SEASON: April to end October
PUBLICATIONS: Section in property guidebook
ROUTES: Free wandering
FACILITIES: Tea-room, WCs, shop
FACILITIES FOR DISABLED VISITORS: Wheelchair access. Motorised buggy available. Guide dogs admitted
LOCATION: 4½m E of Droitwich
OTHER GARDENS IN AREA: Packwood House, Baddesley Clinton, Coughton Court, Hidcote Manor Garden, Bredon Springs (not NT), The Priory (not NT), Spetchley Park (not NT), Clack's Farm (not NT), Stone House Cottage Gardens (not NT)

Hidcote Manor Garden

Hidcote Bartrim, nr Chipping Campden, Gloucestershire GL55 6LR
Tel: Mickleton (01386) 438333

SOIL & TERRAIN: alkaline soil. Level site

ALTITUDE: 182m (600ft)
GARDENERS: seven

Ten-acre Arts and Crafts garden on hilltop created from 1907 onwards by Lawrence Johnston (1871–1958), a superb plantsman and horticulturist. Blend of ordered formality with apparent artlessness of cottage garden. Variously shaped compartments divided by 'tapestry' hedges or yew. Central axis from manor house includes the famous Red Borders, ogival-roofed pavilions painted inside by Johnston and the Stilt Walk (pleached hornbeams) culminating in dramatic view over the Vale of Evesham. Rare shrubs, trees, herbaceous borders, old roses and interesting plant varieties – some, such as *Verbena* 'Lawrence Johnston' and *Hypericum* 'Hidcote', bearing the Hidcote or Johnston names – were developed here.

BEST TIMES TO VISIT: No single best time, good at all seasons. Avoid peak holiday period and Bank Holiday weekends
SEASON: April to end October (closed Tuesdays and Fridays)
PUBLICATIONS: Guidebook. Bird's-eye view garden plan
ROUTES: Free wandering
PLANT SALES: Plant centre adjacent to car park
FACILITIES: Restaurant, WCs, shop, tea bar
FACILITIES FOR DISABLED VISITORS: Access limited in parts for less able due to the nature of some informal stone paved paths. Wheelchair access to part of garden only
LOCATION: 4m NE of Chipping Campden, 1m E of B4632, off B4081 [151:SP176429]
OTHER GARDENS IN AREA: Snowshill Manor, Kiftsgate Court (not NT), Sezincote (not NT), Batsford Arboretum (not NT)

Penrhyn Castle

Bangor, Gwynedd LL57 4HN Tel: Bangor (01248) 353084

SOIL & TERRAIN: sandy and gravelly soil. Thin layer overlying shale and rock. Steep sloping site exposed to prevailing winds

ALTITUDE: 45m (150ft)
GARDENERS: three

Superb site with views to Snowdonia and over Beaumaris Bay. Victorian walled garden containing parterre and terraces with wide collection of climbers and free-standing shrubs: magnolias, camellias, azaleas and fuchsia walk. Lower bog garden with Aralia, tree fern, palms and gunnera. Important collection of trees in grounds including metasequoia and maidenhair tree as well as mature beeches and oaks. Eucryphias and exotic plant collection.

BEST TIMES TO VISIT: Spring to mid summer (but all year interest) for wild flowers and daffodils through to long season of flowering shrubs and plants
SEASON: April to end October
PUBLICATIONS: Garden guide including plan. Also Book of the House with section on grounds
ROUTES: Combination of paths, walks and free wandering
FACILITIES: Tea-room, shop, WCs, adventure playground. Orienteering course
FACILITIES FOR DISABLED VISITORS: Limited wheelchair access to garden (ground floor only of castle). Golf buggy. ♿ WC
LOCATION: 1½m E of Bangor on A5122 [115:SH603720]
OTHER GARDENS IN AREA: Plas Newydd, Bodnant Garden

Plas Newydd

Llanfairpwll, Anglesey, Gwynedd LL61 6EQ
Tel: Llanfairpwll (01248) 714795

SOIL & TERRAIN: acid with some alkaline soil, clay and sandstone overlying limestone. E-sloping site, sheltered by trees from W winds. Coastal location so little frost

ALTITUDE: 30m (100ft)
GARDENERS: three

A parkland garden with some formal areas. Layout based on Humphry Repton's design with sweeping lawns and magnificent woodland. The NT acquired the property in 1976 and continued work of present Marquess of Anglesey, who began to redevelop garden in 1950. Exotic plants thrive in this mild, wet climate. Azaleas, magnolias, Japanese maples and rhododendrons sheltered by belts of trees. A spring garden with fine views to the mountains of Snowdonia. Italianate terrace garden. A recent arboretum of eucalyptus and nothofagus to be kept as a wild flower area. A 5-acre rhododendron wild garden was opened in 1985.

BEST TIMES TO VISIT: Spring display combined with views across Menai Strait to Snowdonia. May to June for rhododendron garden. Autumn colour
SEASON: April to end September
PUBLICATIONS: Garden guide
ROUTES: Paths and free wandering
FACILITIES: Tea-room, shop, WCs, car park, children's play area
FACILITIES FOR DISABLED VISITORS: Slopes but wheelchair access possible to most areas. Some scented shrubs. ♿ WC
LOCATION: E coast of Anglesey on Menai Strait [114 & 115:SH521696]
OTHER GARDENS IN AREA: Penrhyn Castle

Plas-yn-Rhiw

Rhiw, Pwllheli, Gwynedd LL53 8AB Tel: Rhiw (0175 888) 219

SOIL & TERRAIN: acid and light soil. Steeply sloping site overlooking sea, very sheltered, almost frost-free

ALTITUDE: 30m (100ft)

GARDENERS: two part-time

Three-quarter-acre garden overlooking Porth Niegwl on Llyn peninsula. A garden on this site since about 1800, but present garden probably dates from the late 19th century and was restored and replanted in the 1940s – after a long period of neglect – by Eileen, Lorna and Honora Keating. Garden is divided into many sections by box hedges of varying heights and planted mainly with flowering shrubs and trees, ranging from the most ordinary cottage garden plants to the rare and subtropical.

BEST TIMES TO VISIT: April to June for camellias, rhododendrons and azaleas. Can become crowded in August

SEASON: April to end October

ROUTES: Paths throughout garden for free wandering

FACILITIES: WCs

FACILITIES FOR DISABLED VISITORS: Wheelchair access very limited. ♿ WC. Guide dogs admitted

LOCATION: 12m W of Pwllheli on S coast road to Aberdaron [123:SH237282]

OTHER GARDENS IN AREA: Plas Newydd, Penrhyn Castle

Powis Castle

Welshpool, Powys SY21 8RF Tel: Welshpool (01938) 554336

SOIL & TERRAIN: woodland area of 10½ acres acid. Remainder of garden alkaline. Heavy, fertile moisture-retentive soil. Steep and undulating terrain

ALTITUDE: 75m (250ft), but terraces stand 150m (450ft) above sea level

GARDENERS: eight

SPECIAL FEATURES: topiary and hedges, container planting, unusual plants, lush herbaceous and tender perennials, vine arch, woodland garden, tropical and dry plantings on different terraces

Twenty-five-acre garden including an 18th-century Italian-style terraced area, a 19th-century woodland area and a 20th-century Edwardian formal area all planted on different levels. The topiary and hedges unify all these sections and there are many other important features including fine container plantings and the largest collection of herbaceous and tender perennial plants within NT gardens. By making use of microclimate positions a great variety of effects can be achieved, including tropical, arid and luxuriant plantings, all thriving in close proximity to each other. There are spectacular views throughout the garden.

BEST TIMES TO VISIT: Mid June to end October. Busy most days mid July to end August. Avoid Sundays if possible. Meet the Gardener tours available by appointment

SEASON: April to end October

PUBLICATIONS: Separate guidebook to garden. Also garden leaflet giving plan of areas to visit

ROUTES: Free wandering. Paths marked in garden leaflet. Recommended routes for elderly and visitors with disabilities

PLANT SALES: Easter to mid October. Own plants produced and sold by garden staff, including many rare and unusual plants

FACILITIES: Restaurant, tea-room, WCs, shop

FACILITIES FOR DISABLED VISITORS: Access for wheelchairs possible but not easy. ♿ WC. Scented flowers. Guide dogs admitted

LOCATION: Mid Wales, 4m from English border, direct route from Shrewsbury or Oswestry [126:SJ216064]

OTHER GARDENS IN AREA: Chirk Castle, Erddig

Snowshill Manor

nr Broadway, Gloucestershire WR12 7JU
Tel: Broadway (01386) 852410

SOIL & TERRAIN: lime, light soil. Sheltered and sloping site
ALTITUDE: 228m (750ft)
GARDENERS: one

The garden at Snowshill Manor was laid out by Arts and Crafts Movement architect Charles Wade to basic design of M. H. Baillie Scott in the early 1920s on the site of an old farmyard. He built the walls and excavated and levelled the ground to produce different terraces, incorporating existing trees and buildings to create a series of old-world cottage gardens or outdoor rooms embellished with painted and gilded carved ornaments. Stone paths, lawns and borders of herbs, shrubs and perennial plants of great character and variety. A spring rises under the house and Charles Wade used it to create the water features. Organic gardening practised.

BEST TIMES TO VISIT: June for colour and herbs. Garden gets overcrowded at Bank Holidays
SEASON: April to end October
PUBLICATIONS: Section in guidebook to property
ROUTES: Free wandering with paths
FACILITIES: WCs, shop
FACILITIES FOR DISABLED VISITORS: Guide dogs admitted. Scented plants
LOCATION: 3m SW of Broadway [150:SP096339]
OTHER GARDENS IN AREA: Sezincote (not NT), Kiftsgate (not NT), Batsford Arboretum (not NT), Barnsley House Gardens (not NT), Bourton House (not NT), Brook Cottage, Alkerton (not NT), Spetchley Park (not NT), Bredon Springs (not NT), Misarden Park Gardens (not NT), Coughton Court, Charlecote Park, Upton House, Hidcote Manor Garden

The Weir

Swainshill, nr Hereford Tel: (01684) 850051

SOIL & TERRAIN: alkaline, light soil. Steep S-facing slope. Very warm and sheltered

ALTITUDE: 60.9m (200ft)
GARDENERS: two

Situated on steeply sloping south-facing bank on bend of the River Wye, part of Weir Estate given to the NT by Roger Parr, who created the garden in 1920s. Informal garden and riverside walk with small rockery. Mosaic of woodland and open glades, steep terraces and steps; superb views over River Wye and to Black Mountains. Especially attractive in spring. Rustic hut and boat house. River bank shows Roman masonry *in situ*, probably a quay or even bridge abutments.

BEST TIMES TO VISIT: Very early spring garden. Good views all year round
SEASON: Mid February to end October
PUBLICATIONS: Leaflet
ROUTES: Many paths, shown in leaflet
FACILITIES: Car park
FACILITIES FOR DISABLED VISITORS: Unsuitable for wheelchairs. Guide dogs admitted, but please note very steep paths and steps which could be dangerous
LOCATION: 5m W of Hereford [149:SO435419]
OTHER GARDENS IN AREA: Berrington Hall, Lower Brockhampton, Croft Castle, Croft Ambrey (not NT), Hergest Croft Gardens (not NT), Abbey Dore Court (not NT)

Westbury Court Garden

Westbury-on-Severn, Gloucestershire GL14 1PD
Tel: Westbury-on-Severn (01452) 760461

SOIL & TERRAIN: alkaline, medium soil. Flat site susceptible to flooding
ALTITUDE: 9m (30ft)
GARDENERS: one
SPECIAL FEATURES: espaliered fruit trees (16th- and 17th-century varieties), topiary, canals, parterre and pavilions

Walled 4-acre Dutch-style water garden reflecting mania for Dutch fashion in late 17th century. Created between 1696 and 1714 by local gentleman, Maynard Colchester, and his nephew. Escaped 'natural landscaping' of 18th and 19th centuries but overgrown and derelict when the NT acquired it in 1967. Accurate restoration made possible by existence of detailed accounts and contemporary bird's-eye view by Johannes Kip. Where original species no longer available similar 17th-century species have been chosen. Varieties include the culinary pear 'Bellisime d'Hiver' and the apples 'Devonshire Quarrenden' and 'Catshead'. Best surviving example in England of this type of garden.

BEST TIMES TO VISIT: Spring for bulbs and blossom. Summer for display in the walled garden and parterre. Autumn for fruit
PUBLICATIONS: Garden guidebook
ROUTES: Free wandering
FACILITIES: WC, picnic area
FACILITIES FOR DISABLED VISITORS: Wheelchair access. Guide dogs admitted
LOCATION: 9m SW of Gloucester on A48 [162:SO718138]
OTHER GARDENS IN AREA: The Weir, How Caple Court Gardens (not NT), Misarden Garden (not NT), Hill Court Gardens (not NT), Painswick Park (not NT), The Priory at Kemerton (not NT)

London, Thames Valley and the Chilterns

BEDFORDSHIRE · BERKSHIRE · BUCKINGHAMSHIRE
OXFORDSHIRE · LONDON

Ascott

Wing, nr Leighton Buzzard, Buckinghamshire LU7 OPS
Tel: Aylesbury (01296) 688242

SOIL & TERRAIN: limy soil. Terraced terrain
ALTITUDE: 75m (250ft)
GARDENERS: nine full-time; three part-time

SPECIAL FEATURES: terraced gardens, interesting trees and shrubs, water-lily pond

Rothschild house surrounded by garden combining Victorian formality with early 20th-century natural style. Extensive Victorian gardens were laid out by the leading Chelsea nursery of James Veitch and Sons using plants and trees which would be of interest during winter months when the family used the house as a hunting lodge. Terraced lawns with panoramic views to the Chilterns planted with specimen and ornamental trees such as weeping copper beech and juniper. Clipped yew hedges and a retaining wall hide a formal garden including a circular lawn with fountain of Venus in her chariot and a long, narrow Dutch garden with circular beds of annuals. Impressive topiary throughout including giant sundial of box and golden yew. At the far side of the house is a beech hedge avenue leading to a large water-lily lake under restoration.

BEST TIMES TO VISIT: Interesting all year. Good in spring for bulbs and summer for water-lilies
SEASON: April to September
PUBLICATIONS: Section in Book of the House
ROUTES: Free wandering
FACILITIES: WC

FACILITIES FOR DISABLED VISITORS: Limited wheelchair access to garden. Guide dogs admitted
LOCATION: ½m E of Wing, 2m SW of Leighton Buzzard on S side of A418 [165:SP891230]
OTHER GARDENS IN AREA: Stowe Landscape Gardens, Waddesdon Manor

Cliveden

Taplow, Maidenhead, Berkshire SL6 0JA
Tel: Burnham (01628) 605069

SOIL & TERRAIN: alkaline soil, gravel overlaying chalk. Some clay outcrops. Escarpment overlooking Thames Valley. Mostly exposed site

ALTITUDE: 75m (250ft)
GARDENERS: nine

Large 18th-century landscape magnificently sited high on escarpment overlooking Thames Valley. Contains a sequence of historical garden styles: early amphitheatre of 1723 and avenues and rides by Charles Bridgeman; temple and pavilion by Giacomo Leoni; late 18th-century informal rides and viewpoints; parterre from 18th-century French design, famous from 1850s when planted in Victorian manner by John Fleming who developed here the system of biannual displays of bedding plants; Long Garden with topiary and hedges of 1900; wall shrubs, herbaceous borders in Gertrude Jekyll style; Water Garden in eastern style from 1900; Glade Garden designed by Geoffrey Jellicoe 1959, planted with shrub roses. Fountains, sculpture and statuary mostly introduced by Astor family from 1894. Woodland walks and views of 1⅓ miles of river frontage.

BEST TIMES TO VISIT: Spring for bulbs and spring flowering shrubs. Summer for herbaceous borders. Autumn for colours of foliage. Busy at fine weekends and Bank Holidays
SEASON: March to December
PUBLICATIONS: Guidebook with plan. Estate plan leaflet (bird's-eye view) with key routes indicated

ROUTES: Free wandering, but dog routes indicated in woodland on estate map
PLANT SALES: Occasional, limited sale of surplus plants
FACILITIES: Restaurant, WCs, car park, shop
FACILITIES FOR DISABLED VISITORS: Wheelchair access to most areas and recommended routes available. Wheelchairs and motorised buggy available on loan. Guide dogs admitted. Scented plants
LOCATION: 2m N of Taplow, 3m upstream from Maidenhead [175:SU915851]
OTHER GARDENS IN AREA: Dorneywood, Greys Court, Basildon Park, Waddesdon Manor, Osterley, Hughenden Manor, West Wycombe Park, Stowe Landscape Gardens, Savill Garden (not NT), Valley Gardens, Frogmore (not NT), The Old Rectory, Burghfield (not NT), Royal Botanic Gardens, Kew (not NT)

Fenton House

Windmill Hill, Hampstead, London NW3 6RT Tel: 0171-435 3471

SOIL & TERRAIN: neutral, light soil. Terraced garden. Sheltered site
ALTITUDE: 100m (330ft)
GARDENERS: one
SPECIAL FEATURES: herbaceous borders, rose garden, herb border, orchard, kitchen garden

Small walled and terraced garden of 17th-century Hampstead house. Seasonal herbaceous borders edged with box. Some borders feature scented herbs and perennials such as rosemary, lavender and dianthus. Sunken rose garden provides colourful display in summer. Orchard contains mature fruit trees underplanted with spring bulbs. Recently reinstated espaliered trees surround the kitchen garden which contains a wide selection of vegetables.

BEST TIMES TO VISIT: Spring for spring flowers and blossom in orchard, also spring border. Summer for herbaceous borders, rose garden and maturing vegetables. Autumn for fruit
SEASON: March to end October
ROUTES: Free wandering on paths throughout garden

FACILITIES: WC
FACILITIES FOR DISABLED VISITORS: Garden not recommended for wheelchair users due to terracing and steps. Scented roses and herbs. Guide dogs admitted
LOCATION: W side of Hampstead Grove NW3 [176:TQ262860]
OTHER GARDENS IN AREA: Kenwood (not NT), Queen Mary's Rose Garden (not NT), various London parks and squares

Greys Court

Rotherfield Greys, Henley-on-Thames, Oxfordshire RG9 4PG
Tel: Rotherfield Greys (014917) 529

SOIL & TERRAIN: limy soil. Mainly level terrain
ALTITUDE: 75m (250ft)
GARDENERS: two
SPECIAL FEATURES: Archbishop's Maze

Brick and flint Tudor house set in courtyard of a medieval manor. Romantic remains of the 14th-century fortifications spread throughout grounds, mostly overgrown with climbing plants and forming a series of walled gardens. The Tower Garden features magnolias, Californian tree poppies and other white-flowering plants reflected in a central lily pond. A rose garden is planted with old-fashioned species and leads to a circular walled area enclosing some ancient wisterias. Japanese cherries provide shade for the Fountain Garden built within the walls of an old tithe barn. Kitchen garden replanted in 1980 with Morello cherries and espaliered apples with a border of peonies. Wooden statue of St Fiacre, the patron saint of gardeners, stands at end of one path flanked by Rosa Mundi in commemoration of Charles Taylor, the head gardener from 1937–55 who saved the garden from ruin. Beyond the kitchen garden is the brick-paved Archbishop's Maze, the design of which was inspired by Dr Robert Runcie's address at his enthronement as Archbishop of Canterbury in 1980.

BEST TIMES TO VISIT: Spring for magnolias and cherry blossom. Summer for rose garden
SEASON: April to end September
PUBLICATIONS: Section in property guidebook

ROUTES: Free wandering throughout garden
FACILITIES: Teas, WCs
FACILITIES FOR DISABLED VISITORS: Guide dogs admitted. Rose and wisteria garden and banks of rosemary and lavender
LOCATION: 3m W of Henley-on-Thames [175:SU725834]
OTHER GARDENS IN AREA: Cliveden, Hughenden Manor, West Wycombe Park

Hughenden Manor

High Wycombe, Buckinghamshire HP14 4LA
Tel: High Wycombe (01494) 532580

SOIL & TERRAIN: limy soil. Level terrain
ALTITUDE: 152m (500ft)
GARDENERS: one

Five-acre high-Victorian garden surrounding Disraeli's house and largely created by his wife. Set in a delightfully wooded valley. Garden features terrace decorated with vases to Mrs Disraeli's design. The unusual graft hybrid, × *Laburnocytisus adamii*, grows in the garden. The 1880's formal bedding in the South Garden has been restored. The Orchard has been recreated stocking 35 different varieties of old apples and four varieties of pears.

BEST TIMES TO VISIT: Attractive throughout season
SEASON: March to end October
PUBLICATIONS: Section in property guidebook
ROUTES: Paths in garden. Walks in surrounding woodland
FACILITIES: Shop, WCs
FACILITIES FOR DISABLED VISITORS: Garden can be viewed by wheelchair users from terrace. ♿WC
LOCATION: 1½m N of High Wycombe, on W side of Great Missenden road (A4128) [165:SU866955]
OTHER GARDENS IN AREA: Cliveden, West Wycombe Park

Osterley Park

Isleworth, Middlesex TW7 4RB
Tel: 0181-560 3918

SOIL & TERRAIN: lime-free, gravel in some areas, clay in others. Level terrain
ALTITUDE: 30m (100ft)
GARDENERS: six
SPECIAL FEATURES: Hungary and Turkey oaks, Daimyo oak, hickories

Delightful 142-acre, 18th-century park with mansion dating back to Elizabethan times. Given to the NT by the Earl of Jersey in 1949. Well known for its fine specimens of trees (particularly oaks) including *Quercus cerris*, *Quercus frainetto*, Turkey and Hungary oaks. Extensive restoration project undertaken in last few years. Fine temple and garden house designed by Robert Adam (orangery also designed by Adam destroyed in Second World War). Garden lost over 200 trees in the storm of 1987 and 1990 necessitating extensive replanting. Paths through south and west woods and pleasure grounds.

BEST TIMES TO VISIT: Spring months with bluebells in woods, wild grasses. Also good autumn colours. Busiest on summer Sundays and Bank Holidays
SEASON: All year
FACILITIES: Tea-room, shop, WCs
FACILITIES FOR DISABLED VISITORS: Wheelchair access. Motorised buggies available in summer months (by prior arrangement). ♿WC. Guide dogs admitted
LOCATION: N of Osterley London Underground station (Piccadilly line); access from Syon Lane, N side of Great West Road (A4), or from Thornbury Road (¼m E of station) [176:TQ146780]
OTHER GARDENS IN AREA: Cliveden, Fenton House

Stowe Landscape Gardens

Buckingham, Buckinghamshire MK18 5EH
Tel: Buckingham (01280) 822850

SOIL & TERRAIN: lime-free gravel. Undulating terrain
ALTITUDE: 90m (310ft)
GARDENERS: five full-time; one maintenance man; four trainees
SPECIAL FEATURES: temples and eye-catchers

Stowe – probably the most important landscape garden in Britain – came to the NT in 1989. Throughout the 18th century the Temple family employed many of the leading architects, landscape gardeners and sculptors of the day – including Vanbrugh, Bridgeman, Kent and Brown – to create an idealised classical landscape for their country seat in the heart of the Buckinghamshire countryside. Decorated with temples, columns and arches, the Stowe landscape evokes the classical world, so admired by the Georgians. Initially formal in design, Stowe pioneered the revolution towards the more naturalistic landscape of grassy vistas and informal planting perpetuated by Capability Brown, head gardener at Stowe from 1741. The many temples and buildings include the Temple of British Worthies, a Palladian bridge and the Temple of Venus, while different areas of the garden, such as the Elysian Fields and the Grecian Valley, demonstrate the theme of classicism through their titles.

BEST TIMES TO VISIT: All year
SEASON: During school holidays, telephone for dates
PUBLICATIONS: Leaflet. *Descriptions of Lord Cobham's Gardens at Stowe 1700–1750* ed. G. Clarke. *Temples of Delight* by John Martin Robinson (National Trust/Pitkin)
ROUTES: Suggested visitor routes given in leaflet
FACILITIES: Light refreshments during spring and summer holidays
FACILITIES FOR DISABLED VISITORS: Motorised buggy available for loan
LOCATION: 3m NW of Buckingham via Stowe Avenue off A422 Buckingham–Banbury road [152:SP665366]
OTHER GARDENS IN AREA: Waddesdon Manor, Claydon House

Waddesdon Manor

Waddesdon, nr Aylesbury, Buckinghamshire HP18 0JH
Tel: Aylesbury (01296) 651211

SOIL & TERRAIN: alkaline soil. Exposed hilltop site
ALTITUDE: 75m (250ft)
GARDENERS: eight

SPECIAL FEATURES: specimen trees, shrubs, raised Victorian bedding, spring bulbs. Aviary, parterres, statuary, fountains

French Renaissance-style chateau set in 165 acres of parkland and formal gardens. Created by Baron Ferdinand de Rothschild in the 1880s from a bare hilltop site. Paths and roads blend with the contours and the banks are planted with semi-mature trees and underplanted with drifts of shrubs. Outstanding collection of sculpture and two ornamental fountains. Bequeathed to the NT in 1957 by the late James de Rothschild. Ornamental aviary of filigree cast iron has recently been restored. The types of rare and exotic birds in the aviary today are similar to those which the Baron would have kept 100 years ago. The Aviary Garden consists of 'Iceberg' rose beds, lawn and raised bedding within hornbeam hedges. The Fountain Terrace is bedded out in spring with wallflowers and tulips and in summer with geranium and ageratum. A major restoration programme to return the gardens to their Victorian glory was started in 1990.

BEST TIMES TO VISIT: Spring for bulb display. Summer for terrace bedding. If possible avoid Bank Holidays
SEASON: April to October
PUBLICATIONS: Garden guide and leaflet
ROUTES: Paths for free wandering through garden and grounds
FACILITIES: Tea-room, shop, WCs
FACILITIES FOR DISABLED VISITORS: Wheelchair access not easy owing to gravel paths. ♿ WC
LOCATION: 6m NW of Aylesbury on A41, 11m SE of Bicester [165:SP740169]
OTHER GARDENS IN AREA: Cliveden, West Wycombe Park, Hughenden Manor, Claydon House, Stowe Landscape Gardens

West Wycombe Park

West Wycombe, Buckinghamshire HP14 3AJ
Tel: High Wycombe (01494) 524411

SOIL & TERRAIN: limy soil. Valley site
ALTITUDE: 75m (250ft)
GARDENERS: one full-time; one part-time
SPECIAL FEATURES: follies and temples

Forty-six-acre 18th-century landscape garden, largely created by the second Sir Francis Dashwood in the 1730s inspired by his Grand Tours to the Continent. The house and garden are sited in a valley with a dammed river forming lake and cascade. Garden contains series of classical temples and follies, some of which were designed by Nicholas Revett including a cottage disguised as a church. The present baronet has recently added three more eye-catchers designed by Quinlan Terry.

BEST TIMES TO VISIT: Something of interest all season
SEASON: April to end August
PUBLICATIONS: Guidebook to house and garden
ROUTES: Free wandering in garden
FACILITIES: Refreshments at nearby West Wycombe Caves (not NT)
FACILITIES FOR DISABLED VISITORS: Garden partly accessible to wheelchair users. Guide dogs not admitted to park
LOCATION: At W end of West Wycombe, S of Oxford road (A40) [175:SU828947]
OTHER GARDENS IN AREA: Hughenden Manor, Cliveden, Waddesdon Manor, Stowe Landscape Gardens

Heart of England

CHESHIRE · DERBYSHIRE · NOTTINGHAMSHIRE
NORTHAMPTONSHIRE · STAFFORDSHIRE · WARWICKSHIRE
WEST MIDLANDS

Apprentice House Garden

Quarry Bank Mill, Styal, Wilmslow, Cheshire SK9 4LA
Tel: Wilmslow (01625) 527468

SOIL & TERRAIN: acid, heavy soil. Level terrain, sheltered from SW

ALTITUDE: 75m (250ft)

GARDENERS: one full-time; one part-time

Re-creation of a 19th-century kitchen garden of 1½ acres in the grounds of the Apprentice House at Quarry Bank Mill. About 100 children lived in the house and laboured daily in the cotton mill. The garden had to provide food for the hungry children, so nothing exotic or luxurious was and is grown. 19th-century varieties of fruit, vegetables and herbs are grown using methods and materials of the period. Local varieties of fruit and vegetables are also featured, such as 'Early Timperley' rhubarb and 'Withington's Welter' apple – both named after nearby villages.

BEST TIMES TO VISIT: Vegetable garden at its best from June to September. Sunday afternoons and Bank Holidays are very busy

SEASON: All year

PUBLICATIONS: Leaflet with plan of garden

ROUTES: Free wandering. Organised tours/talks available if required

FACILITIES: Restaurant, WCs, shop at Mill (5-minute walk)

FACILITIES FOR DISABLED VISITORS: Wheelchair access. Guide dogs admitted

LOCATION: 1½m N of Wilmslow off B5166, 1m from M56, junction 5, 10m S of Manchester [109:SJ835835]

OTHER GARDENS IN AREA: Tatton Park, Dunham Massey, Lyme Park, Harehill, Biddulph Grange, Little Moreton Hall

Baddesley Clinton

Knowle, Solihull, Warwickshire B93 0DQ
Tel: Lapworth (01564) 783294

SOIL & TERRAIN: alkaline, heavy soil. Open, gently undulating site

ALTITUDE: 110m (370ft)
GARDENERS: two

Forecourt and walled garden remain from formal setting given to the ancient moated manor house in early 18th century. The Victorians' attempt to give the house a wooded setting partly survives in the rhododendron plantings and the walk around the chain of 15th-century fish ponds. The walled garden formerly divided by yew hedge into vegetable garden and parterre garden was opened into a single space by Thomas Ferrers who came to Baddesley in 1940. Present planting scheme and raised walk formed following acquisition by the NT in 1980. Courtyard garden devised 1890 with Ferrers' arms vividly planted on the lawn. Herbs, moat, ponds and lake.

BEST TIMES TO VISIT: Daffodils in spring provide good display. June to August for border colour. Generally very busy at weekends and Bank Holidays
SEASON: March to end October
ROUTES: Free wandering. Pleasant walk around lake
FACILITIES: Restaurant, shop, WCs
FACILITIES FOR DISABLED VISITORS: Wheelchair access to most of garden. Guide dogs admitted
LOCATION: ¾m W of A41 Warwick–Birmingham road, at Chadwick End, 7½m N of Warwick, 15m SE of central Birmingham [139:SP200715]
OTHER GARDENS IN AREA: Packwood House, Charlecote Park, Coughton Court, Upton House, Farnborough Hall, Warwick Castle (not NT), Castle Bromwich (not NT)

Biddulph Grange Garden

Biddulph, Stoke-on-Trent, Staffordshire ST8 7SD
Tel: Stoke-on-Trent (01782) 517999

SOIL & TERRAIN: acid and light soil. Uneven but sheltered site
ALTITUDE: 150m (450ft)
GARDENERS: four
SPECIAL FEATURES: themed garden featuring variety of gardens within the whole

Fifteen-acre Victorian garden opened for the first time in 1991 after major restoration, which is still taking place. Created between 1846 and 1871 by James Bateman and Edward Cooke, the marine painter. A remarkable survivor of the high-Victorian style, the garden is split into areas: China, Egypt, Dahlia Walk, Arboretum, Pinetum, Rhododendron Ground with a multiplicity of buildings – many of oriental style – tunnels, winding paths and rockwork. Each area of the garden designed for different purposes and to contain specific plants. Highly accurate restoration made possible from drawings, early photographs and descriptions. Replanting of trees, shrubs and plants is taking place with species which either were known to be in the garden or could have been in the garden in the mid nineteenth century. The resulting restoration is the most complete high-Victorian garden in the country.

BEST TIMES TO VISIT: Interesting throughout season
SEASON: April to end October
PUBLICATIONS: Garden plan and leaflet. Colour guide. *Biddulph Grange* by Peter Hayden. *The World in a Garden* video
ROUTES: Paths, free wandering with suggestions of route
FACILITIES: Tea-room, WCs, shop
FACILITIES FOR DISABLED VISITORS: Access difficult for wheelchairs and pushchairs because of steps, and winding paths, but access to tea-room, shop and lawns. Contact Head Gardener for details
LOCATION: 5m E of Congleton, 7m N of Stoke-on-Trent. Access from A527 [118:SJ895591]
OTHER GARDENS IN AREA: Little Moreton Hall, Tatton Park, Hare Hill, Dunham Massey, Lyme Park, Alton Towers (not NT)

Calke Abbey

Ticknall, Derbyshire DE73 1LE Tel: Melbourne (01332) 863822

SOIL & TERRAIN: walled gardens: alkaline soil. Level terrain and sheltered site. Pleasure grounds: acid soil. Undulating terrain, exposed to W winds

ALTITUDE: 120m (400ft)
GARDENERS: two; one trainee

Surrounding the house are the informal pleasure grounds laid out by Sir Harry Harpur and his son, Sir Henry, between about 1770 and 1820. The extensive walled gardens constructed in 1773 lie to the south-east of the house and are divided into the flower garden, the physic garden and the kitchen garden. At present only the flower and physic gardens have been restored and are cultivated, the physic garden being used for a wide range of fruit and vegetables including many old varieties. The centrepiece is the derelict orangery and gardener's bothy (built 1777). Also of interest is the dahlia walk and 19th-century auricula theatre. Beyond the walled gardens, the pleasure grounds have been fenced to exclude deer and allow replanting of shrubs and trees.

BEST TIMES TO VISIT: Mid to late July for annual bedding and vegetables at their best. Suffers from crowding at weekends and Bank Holidays
SEASON: April to end October
PUBLICATIONS: Section in Book of the House. *Calke Abbey: a hidden house revealed* by Howard Colvin (George Philip in association with the NT)
ROUTES: Free wandering
FACILITIES: Restaurant, WCs, shop
FACILITIES FOR DISABLED VISITORS: Accessible but difficult terrain for wheelchairs (some steps). Motorised buggy available. Guide dogs admitted. Scented plants and textured tree bark
LOCATION: 9m S of Derby, on A514 at Ticknall between Swadlincote and Melbourne. Gardens are situated 300 yards from car park [128:SK356239]

OTHER GARDENS IN AREA: Kedleston Hall, Sudbury Hall, Melbourne Hall (not NT)

Canons Ashby House

Daventry, Northamptonshire NN11 6SD
Tel: Blakesley (01327) 860044

SOIL & TERRAIN: neutral, medium to light soil. Gentle slope. Exposed and windy site

ALTITUDE: 150m (500ft)
GARDENERS: one

Formal garden created between 1708 and 1717 by Edward Dryden, at same time as house remodelled. Recognised as one of the best surviving formal layouts in the style of Henry London and George Wise, and a considerable influence on the Lutyens-Gertrude Jekyll generation of gardeners early this century. Derelict and overgrown when house rescued by the NT. Restoration work of 1980s is maturing. Garden divided by stone walls and yew hedges into courts with terraces and topiary. Early 18th-century timber gates and garden seats together with fine cedar of Lebanon. In the Green Court is a lead statue of a shepherd boy attributed to Jan Van Nost (early 18th century). Old fruit varieties including plums, pears and apples of the same varieties as found in the *Mary Rose*. Terracing. Mixed rose and herbaceous borders.

BEST TIMES TO VISIT: Spring for bulbs. Mid summer for colour and roses, but something of interest throughout season
SEASON: April to end October
ROUTES: Free wandering
FACILITIES: Tea-room, WCs, shop
FACILITIES FOR DISABLED VISITORS: Wheelchair access on top terraces. Guide dogs admitted. Guided walks. Scented flowers
LOCATION: 14m SW of Northampton off A361 Daventry–Banbury road [152:SP577506]
OTHER GARDENS IN AREA: Stowe Landscape Gardens, Upton House, Farnborough Hall, Sulgrave Manor (not NT)

Charlecote Park

Wellesbourne, Warwick CV35 9ER
Tel: Stratford-upon-Avon (01789) 470277

SOIL & TERRAIN: acid, light well-drained soil. Exposed site
ALTITUDE: 50m (170ft)
GARDENERS: one

The house lies at the centre of a wooded park and dates from the mid 16th century although it was substantially remodelled in Elizabethan Revival style in the early 19th century. The balustraded formal garden also dates from this time and features clipped yews and terraces with urns planted with geraniums and lobelia. A 19th-century orangery and a rustic thatched summerhouse stand by the Cedar Lawn. Shakespeare is said to have poached deer in Charlecote Park and a border close to the orangery has been planted with species mentioned in his plays, such as columbine, dog violets and cuckoo flower. The Ladies' Walk, on a raised promontory with fine park views and vistas to two churches, was built in the 19th century by the Lucy family. The park, remodelled by Capability Brown, includes a cascade south of the house, created by altering the course of the River Dene.

BEST TIMES TO VISIT: Spring for bulbs. Summer for colour
SEASON: April to end October
PUBLICATIONS: Section in guidebook. Park walk leaflet
ROUTES: Free wandering
FACILITIES: Restaurant, WCs, shop
FACILITIES FOR DISABLED VISITORS: Wheelchair access to most of garden. Guide dogs admitted
LOCATION: 1m W of Wellesbourne, 5m E of Stratford-upon-Avon, 6m S of Warwick [151:SP263564]
OTHER GARDENS IN AREA: Baddesley Clinton, Packwood House, Coughton Court, Hidcote Manor Garden, Upton House, Farnborough Hall, Kiftsgate Court, Chipping Campden (not NT), Batsford Park Arboretum, Moreton-in-Marsh (not NT), Sezincote, Bourton House, Bourton-on-the-Hill (not NT), Brook Cottage, Alkerton, Banbury (not NT)

Clumber Park

Worksop, Nottinghamshire S80 3AZ Tel: Worksop (01909) 476592

SOIL & TERRAIN: acid, light soil. Level terrain. Frequently subjected to ground frost

ALTITUDE: 30m (100ft)
GARDENERS: two

Informal pleasure grounds around site of house (demolished in 1938) laid out in the 19th century, planted with rhododendrons and specimen trees and including the formal Lincoln Terrace next to the lake. A cedar-lined walk connects the pleasure gardens to the extensive 18th-century walled kitchen gardens with magnificent vineries and palm house added in the 19th century. Part of the walled gardens, including the vineries, are open to the public as a museum of 19th-century kitchen gardening, with exhibition of tools, potting shed, apple store and gardeners' mess room. Within the park are various 18th-century landscape garden buildings including two temples and an elegant bridge. Fine Gothic Revival chapel completed 1889 surrounded by rhododendrons, shrubs and wide variety of trees. The double lime avenue is particularly fine.

BEST TIMES TO VISIT: May to June for rhododendrons. Autumn for tree colour. Crowded at Bank Holidays and summer Sundays
SEASON: All year
PUBLICATIONS: Map and guide covering whole park
ROUTES: Free wandering
PLANT SALES: Plant centre near clocktower shop
FACILITIES: Restaurant, WCs, shop
FACILITIES FOR DISABLED VISITORS: Wheelchairs available. Good access
LOCATION: 4½m SE of Worksop, 6½m SW of Retford [120:SK645774]
OTHER GARDENS IN AREA: Hardwick Hall, Newstead Abbey (not NT)

Dunham Massey

Altrincham, Cheshire WA14 4SJ Tel: 0161-941 1025

SOIL & TERRAIN: acid loamy sand with high water table. Level and sheltered, mild winters but late frosts
ALTITUDE: 25m (85ft)
GARDENERS: five

SPECIAL FEATURES: moat, mount, parterre, arbour, orangery, lake, waterside plantings. Mixed shrub and herbaceous borders. Fine lawns. Late-flowering azaleas. Herbaceous waterside planting

Twenty-acre informal garden, essentially Victorian/Edwardian in style, but with mount, moat and orangery reflecting over 400 years of landscape history, and well represented in paintings by Kip and Knyff in the house. Acquired in 1976 in a largely overgrown and neglected state since the Second World War, the NT, with few existing records, has extensively replanted the garden with mixed borders, good ground cover and a wide range of shrubs and herbaceous plants on a large scale. The Trust has also added waterside, courtyard and woodland plantings, renovated the 4 acres of fine lawns and resurfaced and relaid serpentine paths. It now represents a fine example of a mature garden's evolution and recovery, and reflects the changing tastes of the past 100 years.

BEST TIMES TO VISIT: May to September for azaleas, herbaceous borders, hydrangeas. Garden only crowded on Bank Holidays
SEASON: April to October
PUBLICATIONS: Garden leaflet. Colour souvenir to property
ROUTES: Wide, flat gravel paths for free wandering
PLANT SALES: Plant sales on special occasions
FACILITIES: Restaurant, tea-room, shop, WCs
FACILITIES FOR DISABLED VISITORS: Good access for wheelchairs (no steps). Paths adjacent to borders for scent and texture. Access on grass only for north side of garden
LOCATION: 3m SW of Altrincham off A56 [109:SJ735874]
OTHER GARDENS IN AREA: Tatton Park, Arley Hall (not NT), Hare Hill, Capesthorne Hall (not NT), Lyme Park

Farnborough Hall

Banbury, Oxfordshire OX17 1DU Tel: (01295 89) 202

SOIL & TERRAIN: loam with clay beneath. Sheltered site

ALTITUDE: 150m (500ft)

GARDENERS: one

Untouched 18th-century elysium devised by William Holbech about 1745 with advice from Sanderson Miller who lived nearby. Series of pools adapted from a string of stewponds. Cascade. $\frac{2}{3}$m Terrace Walk in ascending, serpentine curve starts from house, punctuated by Ionic temple and oval temple and terminating with an obelisk. Panoramic views from the temples. Precursor by 6 years of Rievaulx Terrace (see p.125). Rose garden. The Farnborough landscape, including William Holbech's house, passed to the NT in 1960.

BEST TIMES TO VISIT: April for daffodils. June to September for roses and flowers in urns
SEASON: April to end September
PUBLICATIONS: Section in property guidebook
ROUTES: Free wandering during open hours only
FACILITIES: WCs
FACILITIES FOR DISABLED VISITORS: Limited wheelchair access. Guide dogs admitted
LOCATION: 6m N of Banbury, $\frac{1}{2}$m W of A423 [151:SP430490]
OTHER GARDENS IN AREA: Upton House, Hidcote Manor, Charlecote Park, Canons Ashby, Stowe Landscape Gardens, Kiftsgate (not NT), Batsford (not NT), Brook Cottage, Alkerton (not NT), Broughton Castle (not NT)

Hardwick Hall

Doe Lea, Chesterfield, Derbyshire S44 5QJ
Tel: Chesterfield (01246) 850430

SOIL & TERRAIN: alkaline soil. Level terrain, sited on top of a magnesium limestone escarpment. Within courtyards subject to wind
ALTITUDE: 200m (600ft)
GARDENERS: four; two trainees

SPECIAL FEATURES: lead statues in yew alcoves. Holly domes to the western entrance to herb garden. Extensive herb garden, mainly culinary but with some medicinal and dye plants. Grass walks. Yew and hornbeam hedges, mulberry avenue. National Collection of *Scabiosa caucasica*

Only walls and gazebos remain from Bess of Hardwick's late 16th-century garden. Present layout of south garden dates from 1870s: grass alleys flanked by yew and hornbeam hedges planted by Lady Louisa Egerton, daughter of 7th Duke of Devonshire, divide the garden into quadrants. Orchards, lawns, nuttery and herb garden occupy these four sections, conveying the spirit of an Elizabethan garden. West courtyard laid out *c.*1920 by Blanche, 6th Duke's niece. The Duchess Evelyn, wife of the 9th Duke, sank the pond in the East Court to provide water for fire fighting. She also planted the double avenue called 'the wineglass' that closes the eastern vista.

BEST TIMES TO VISIT: Spring for daffodils in the orchard. Early summer for roses and herb garden. Late summer and autumn for the West Court borders. Garden subject to crowding on summer Sundays and Bank Holidays
SEASON: April to end October
PUBLICATIONS: Herb garden guide. Section in Book of the House guidebook
ROUTES: Free wandering
PLANT SALES: Small-scale garden barrow sales at weekends and Bank Holidays from mid April to end October selling excess plants (mainly herbs)
FACILITIES: Restaurant, WCs, shop

FACILITIES FOR DISABLED VISITORS: Garden and some parts of park accessible. ♿ WC. Guide dogs admitted. Scented plants and textured tree bark

LOCATION: 6½m W of Mansfield, 9½m SE of Chesterfield, approach from M1 (junction 29) via A6175 [120:SK463638]

OTHER GARDENS IN AREA: Clumber Park, Kedleston Hall, Haddon Hall (not NT), Chatsworth House (not NT), Newstead Abbey (not NT)

Hare Hill Garden

Prestbury Road, Over Alderley, nr Macclesfield, Cheshire SK10 4QB

SOIL & TERRAIN: slowly permeable fine clayey loams subject to seasonal waterlogging. Level terrain

ALTITUDE: 150m (500ft)

GARDENERS: one

SPECIAL FEATURES: many varieties of species including rhododendrons, azaleas, an exceptionally fine collection of hollies, hosta beds and a rockery. Walled garden with statues. Pergola

Ten-acre garden including a walled area laid out at the same time as Hare Hill was built *c.*1820, though the main developments in the walled garden took place in the latter part of the 19th century. The area around the walled garden, although planted with some exotic species in the 19th century, was mainly developed this century by Colonel Charles Brocklehurst with advice from James Russell.

BEST TIMES TO VISIT: April to June for rhododendrons and azaleas

SEASON: April to end October

ROUTES: Hard paths and grass paths for free wandering

FACILITIES: WCs

FACILITIES FOR DISABLED VISITORS: Some wheelchair access with assistance. Guide dogs admitted

LOCATION: 1m W of Prestbury, 4m NW of Congleton [118:SJ875765]

OTHER GARDENS IN AREA: Little Moreton Hall, Tatton Park, Lyme Park, Dunham Massey, Biddulph Grange

Kedleston Hall

Derby, Derbyshire DE22 5TH Tel: Derby (01332) 842191

SOIL & TERRAIN: acid, mainly light soil. Level terrain
ALTITUDE: 100m (330ft)
GARDENERS: two

Pleasure grounds and landscape park laid out by 1st Lord Scarsdale with designs and buildings by Robert Adam. A feature is the $3\frac{1}{2}$-mile Long Walk which swings round to the south of the house, giving extensive views. The pleasure grounds underwent some formalisation at the end of the 19th century and between 1922–4 when Edwin Lutyens and Gertrude Jekyll advised. Present planting re-establishes the 18th-century feel of the pleasure grounds. 18th-century garden buildings and monuments, including an orangery (1800–1) and hexagonal summerhouse, lie within the pleasure grounds which are planted with rhododendrons, shrubs and species trees. In the park further landscape/garden buildings, including the bridge and cascade (1770–1) together with fishing room/boathouse (1770–2), are also the work of Robert Adam.

BEST TIMES TO VISIT: May to June for azaleas and rhododendrons
PUBLICATIONS: Section in property guidebook
ROUTES: Free wandering
FACILITIES: Restaurant, shop, WCs
FACILITIES FOR DISABLED VISITORS: Help with wheelchair access into garden is provided on request. Once in, access for wheelchairs is good
LOCATION: 3m N of Derby [128:SK312403]
OTHER GARDENS IN AREA: Hardwick Hall, Calke Abbey, Sudbury Hall, Melbourne Hall (not NT)

Little Moreton Hall

Congleton, Cheshire CW12 4SD Tel: Congleton (01260) 272018

SOIL & TERRAIN: lime-free soil. Level terrain. N-facing garden, sheltered by yew hedges, surrounded by moat
ALTITUDE: 75m (250ft)
GARDENERS: one

Garden bounded by a moat includes 17th-century-style knot garden and yew tunnel. Herb garden and historic vegetable garden planted with some of the earliest known varieties grown in England eg colewort, salsify, leaf beet, borecole, winter radish, haricot beans and marrowfat peas. Though no record of original gardens exists, layout and planting with period plants complement the remarkable timber-framed moated house.

BEST TIMES TO VISIT: Summer for flowers and vegetables. Can become crowded at Bank Holidays and fine Sundays
SEASON: March to end October
PUBLICATIONS: Section in property guidebook. Leaflet on historic vegetables
ROUTES: Free wandering. Paths follow perimeter of house and moat
PLANT SALES: Sale of herbs
FACILITIES: Tea-room, WCs, shop
FACILITIES FOR DISABLED VISITORS: Wheelchair access. Guide dogs admitted. Motorised buggy. ♿WC
LOCATION: On A34 4m S of Congleton [118:SJ832589]
OTHER GARDENS IN AREA: Biddulph Grange Garden, Tatton Park, Dunham Massey, Speke Hall, Shugborough

Lyme Park

Disley, Stockport, Cheshire SK12 2NX Tel: Disley (01663) 762023

SOIL & TERRAIN: acid, heavy soil. Site slopes from E to W in series of steps
ALTITUDE: 152m (500ft)
GARDENERS: four

Sixteen-acre garden perched in foothills of the Peak District, representing 600 years of ownership by Legh family but largely restored to its mid-Victorian splendour. The skeleton of the formal 17th-century garden survives in terracing to the east, at the top of which lie herbaceous borders replanted to a scheme by Graham Stuart Thomas. Notable for massed formal bedding in the sunken Dutch garden. Bedding often features *Penstemon* 'Rubicunda' bred at Lyme early this century. Lady Newton's Edwardian rose garden replanted 1990. Early 19th-century orangery designed by Lewis Wyatt contains two camellias of unknown provenance planted c.1820. The Killtime Valley is a feature, as are the magnificent views both from the house and from across the lake.

BEST TIMES TO VISIT: Late spring and summer for bedding due to altitude
SEASON: April to October
PUBLICATIONS: Section in property guide. Also *History of Gardens of Lyme* and *Companion to Gardens of Lyme*
ROUTES: Numerous paths and steps, free wandering
FACILITIES: Tea-room and shop when Hall open
FACILITIES FOR DISABLED VISITORS: Very difficult terrain, only limited access for wheelchairs. Guide dogs admitted
LOCATION: On S side of A6 Manchester–Buxton road ½m W of Disley village [109:SJ965825]
OTHER GARDENS IN AREA: Tatton Park, Dunham Massey, Arley Hall (not NT), Haddon Hall (not NT), Hare Hill

Moseley Old Hall

Moseley Old Hall Lane, Fordhouses, Wolverhampton WV10 7HY
Tel: Wolverhampton (01902) 782808

SOIL & TERRAIN: heavy, neutral soil. Flat terrain. Walled garden, fairly sheltered
ALTITUDE: 75m (250ft)
GARDENERS: one part-time

One-acre 17th-century-style garden planted only with species known to have existed in England before 1700. The house sheltered Charles II for two days after his disastrous defeat at Worcester in 1651. Main feature is knot garden from a design of 1640 by Rev. Walter Stonehouse of Darfield, Yorkshire. The pattern is of dwarf box infilled with coloured gravels. Also a wooden arbour trained with clematis and vines. The arbour leads into a nut walk then to the King's Gate by the orchard.

BEST TIMES TO VISIT: All year interest. Spring for bulbs. Summer for roses and herbaceous borders
SEASON: Mid March to end October
PUBLICATIONS: Garden guide with plan of main features
ROUTES: Paths and limited free wandering

PLANT SALES: Limited plant sales, mainly herbs
FACILITIES: Tea-room, WCs
FACILITIES FOR DISABLED VISITORS: Wheelchair access to most parts of garden and tea-room. ♿ WC. Guide dogs admitted. Scented plants, herbs and roses (June to July)
LOCATION: 4m N of Wolverhampton, S of M54 between Junctions 1 and 2 [127:SJ932044]
OTHER GARDENS IN AREA: Wightwick Manor, Dudmaston, Benthall Hall

Packwood House

Lapworth, Solihull, Warwickshire B94 6AT
Tel: Lapworth (01564) 782024

SOIL & TERRAIN: alkaline, heavy soil. Gently sloping and exposed site
ALTITUDE: 120m (396ft)
GARDENERS: two permanent; two trainees

Seven-acre Grade I listed garden with famous yew garden said to represent 'The Sermon on the Mount', originally set out by John Fetherston *c.*1650–1670. A large single yew set on a tall mound is reached by a spiral path, with 12 large yew trees on the terrace below. Many more yews, representing the multitude, were planted below in the 1850s in what was once the orchard. The 17th-century terraced raised walk is reached via semi-circular brick steps, with an 18th-century wrought iron gate at the top. Set into the wall on one side are 'bee boles' used for housing woven bee hives. Caroline garden beside the house enclosed by 17th-century brick walls with gazebos at each corner. Fine herbaceous mixed borders set out in 19th-century arrangement along many walls of the Caroline garden, raised garden and around sunken pool. Interesting features include two Roman baths and sundials.

BEST TIMES TO VISIT: June to August for herbaceous borders
SEASON: April to end October
PUBLICATIONS: Section in guidebook to property
ROUTES: New woodland and parkland walks
FACILITIES: Small shop, WCs

FACILITIES FOR DISABLED VISITORS: Wheelchair access to main garden. Guide dogs admitted
LOCATION: 11m SE of Birmingham, 2m E of Hockley Heath
OTHER GARDENS IN AREA: Baddesley Clinton, Charlecote Park, Coughton Court, Upton House, Farnborough Hall, Castle Bromwich (not NT)

Shugborough

Milford, nr Stafford ST17 0XB Tel: Little Haywood (01889) 881388

SOIL & TERRAIN: acid, light soil. Level, exposed site
ALTITUDE: 30m (100ft)
GARDENERS: three

SPECIAL FEATURES: Chinese house (*c*.1747), architectural monuments. Mass planting on terraces of yellow roses and lavender. Victorian-style rose garden, layered yew tree covering an area of approximately ½ an acre

Twenty-acre landscape garden of the ancestral home of the Earls of Lichfield laid out in the mid 1700s. Important Neo-classical buildings and monuments, principally by Thomas Wright and James 'Athenian' Stuart, and many fine trees both within the garden and in the adjoining 1,000-acre parkland. During the late 19th century the garden in front of the house was redesigned by W. A. Nesfield into a series of terraced lawns with stone urns and troughs and now a colour scheme of lavender, yellow roses and grey foliage is predominant. Adjacent to the terraces is a Victorian-style rose garden. Remaining areas are planted with rhododendrons and a variety of shrubs and ground-cover plants. New herbaceous border, 140 feet long, planted in 1991, and over the next few years a number of further improvements will be made.

BEST TIMES TO VISIT: Spring with mass plantings of daffodils, early June for rhododendrons, July for roses and July to September for herbaceous border. Autumn colours. Events programme can result in busy days
SEASON: April to October (January to March booked parties only)

PUBLICATIONS: Section on grounds in Book of the House. Separate guide available for various monuments
ROUTES: Free wandering and woodland walks
FACILITIES: Restaurant, shop, WCs, car parking (charge for all visitors). Also county museum, rare breeds farm with working farm museum and mill
FACILITIES FOR DISABLED VISITORS: Wheelchair access. ♿ WC. Guide dogs admitted. Textured tree bark. In early summer azaleas and osmanthus are very fragrant and in July the Victorian-style rose garden is filled with scent
LOCATION: 6m E of Stafford on A513 [127:SJ992225]
OTHER GARDENS IN AREA: Biddulph Grange, Moseley Old Hall, Wightwick Manor, Wolsey Garden Park (not NT), Hodnet Hall (not NT), Dorothy Clive Garden (not NT)

Tatton Park

Knutsford, Cheshire WA16 6QN Tel: Knutsford (01565) 654822/3

SOIL & TERRAIN: acid soil. Open site
ALTITUDE: 60.9m (200ft)
GARDENERS: thirteen
SPECIAL FEATURES: fernery, Japanese garden, small beech maze

The 60 acres of garden to the south of the house bear the strong mark of the Egerton family, the last four generations of whom can be accredited with most of the present planting. In 1814 Lewis Wyatt designed the conservatory (fully restored and planted in 1994). In 1859 Joseph Paxton was engaged to construct the Italian garden and the fernery. Fernery contains huge examples of New Zealand tree ferns. Lord Egerton's wife, Lady Charlotte, converted a disused marl pit into a lake named the Golden Brook. The pinetum was planted from 1883–1909 leaving a framework for the Japanese garden planted with maples, dwarf conifers, Kurume azaleas and evergreens. The fourth and last Egerton was responsible for most of the rhododendron planting from 1920–58. Restoration of the walled garden is underway.

BEST TIMES TO VISIT: May for rhododendrons. October for autumn colours

SEASON: All year
PUBLICATIONS: Garden guide
ROUTES: Free wandering
PLANT SALES: Small-scale plant sales when garden is open
FACILITIES: Restaurant, shop, WCs, car park
FACILITIES FOR DISABLED VISITORS: Wheelchair access to most of garden. Motorised buggy. Wheelchairs available. Guide dogs admitted
LOCATION: Signposted from junction 19 of M6 and junction 7 of M56, off main A556 and A5034 [109 & 118:SJ745815]
OTHER GARDENS IN AREA: Dunham Massey, Hare Hill, Arley Hall (not NT)

Upton House

Banbury, Oxfordshire OX15 6HT Tel: Edge Hill (01295) 87266

SOIL & TERRAIN: alkaline, light soil. Valley site with terraces. Moderately exposed, part frost pocket
ALTITUDE: 213m (700ft)
GARDENERS: five

An intensively planted and manicured garden created by the 2nd Lord Bearsted after 1927, overlaying late 17th-century features. The main garden lies hidden beyond the lawn south of the house and is reached by a grand 20th-century stone staircase by Morley Horder, the architect, who remodelled the house. This leads to a series of terraces housing an NCCPG National Collection of asters with a kitchen garden below, still used for growing fruit and vegetables. This is bounded to the south by a lake, to the east by double herbaceous borders and to the west by two small formal gardens – one a yew – enclosed rose garden, the other (Her Ladyship's Garden) for assorted flowers. Cascades of wisteria and spray roses overhang the terrace. The beds along the south front of the house are planted in blue and yellow. Below the house to the west is a yew walk and bog garden with banqueting pavilion, now a gardener's cottage. Miss K. Lloyd-Jones advised Lady Bearsted on the planting.

BEST TIMES TO VISIT: May for good spring display. June for herbaceous borders. Early autumn for asters

SEASON: April to end October
PUBLICATIONS: Garden leaflet with bird's-eye view
ROUTES: Free wandering
PLANT SALES: Sales of fruit, vegetables and selection of plants
FACILITIES: Tea-room, shop, WCs
FACILITIES FOR DISABLED VISITORS: Motorised buggy and wheelchair access. Guide dogs admitted
LOCATION: On A422, 7m NW of Banbury, 12m SE of Stratford-upon-Avon [151:SP371461]
OTHER GARDENS IN AREA: Farnborough Hall, Hidcote Manor Garden, Canons Ashby, Charlecote Park, Broughton Castle (not NT)

Wightwick Manor

Wightwick Bank, Wolverhampton, West Midlands WV6 8EE
Tel: Wolverhampton (01902) 761108

SOIL & TERRAIN: acid and light soil. Undulating terrain. South sloping site
ALTITUDE: 100m (320ft)
GARDENERS: two; also trainee(s)
SPECIAL FEATURES: avenue of Irish yews and golden hollies. Stones from the House of Commons. A replica of the Mathematical Bridge at Queens' College, Cambridge

Sixteen acres of self-contained landscape in urban setting around late 19th-century house built by Theodore Mander, paint manufacturer and admirer of William Morris. Alfred Parsons RA advised first, subsequently Thomas Mawson whose plan of 1910 was largely implemented, including terrace with characteristic steps and balustrade. Another terrace contains the 'Poets' Garden' with plants from gardens of Shelley, Keats etc. To north-west lies a formal garden of clipped yew, and yew walks lead out to shrubberies, paddocks, trees, streams and two large ponds. Development based on restoration of Mawson plan and inter-war heyday, but with objective of year-round interest.

BEST TIMES TO VISIT: Spring and autumn, but of interest throughout the year. Not heavily visited
SEASON: March to end December

PUBLICATIONS: Garden leaflet
ROUTES: Free wandering
FACILITIES: WCs, tea-room, shop
FACILITIES FOR DISABLED VISITORS: Limited wheelchair access. Guide dogs admitted
LOCATION: 3m W of Wolverhampton, off A454 (Bridgnorth road) [139:SO869985]
OTHER GARDENS IN AREA: Moseley Old Hall, Dudmaston, Shugborough, Wolseley Garden Park (not NT)

Eastern Counties

CAMBRIDGESHIRE · LINCOLNSHIRE
NORFOLK · SUFFOLK

Anglesey Abbey

Lode, Cambridge CB5 9EJ Tel: Cambridge (01223) 811200

SOIL & TERRAIN: limy soil. Level terrain
ALTITUDE: 30m (100ft)
GARDENERS: six
SPECIAL FEATURES: avenues, statuary, unusual trees

Hundred-acre garden developed from 1926 by the 1st Lord Fairhaven presenting an imposing blend of formal 17th-century French-style and 18th-century natural landscaping. Majestic tree-lined avenues and walks form framework for hidden, more formal gardens such as the dahlia garden, hyacinth garden and semi-circular herbaceous garden. Lord Fairhaven's impressive collection of statuary is positioned throughout the grounds and used as features in garden layout. Many rare and unusual tree species planted on arboretum lawns such as Japanese hop hornbeam.

BEST TIMES TO VISIT: Spring for hyacinth garden. Summer for dahlia and herbaceous garden
SEASON: April to end October
PUBLICATIONS: Section in property guidebook. Garden leaflet. *The Gardens of Anglesey Abbey* by Lanning Roper
ROUTES: Walks and avenues integral part of garden design
PLANT SALES: Small plant centre adjacent to shop selling wide variety of plants found at Anglesey Abbey
FACILITIES: Restaurant, shop, picnic area, WCs
FACILITIES FOR DISABLED VISITORS: Good wheelchair access. Guide dogs admitted. Scented hyacinths. ♿ WC. Two motorised buggies
LOCATION: At Lode, 6m NE of Cambridge on B1102 [154:TL533622]
OTHER GARDENS IN AREA: Various Cambridge college gardens, University Botanic Garden, Cambridge (not NT), Ickworth

Belton House

Grantham, Lincolnshire NG32 2LS Tel: Grantham (01476) 66116

SOIL & TERRAIN: acid, light soil. Flat terrain. Exposed site with partial frost pocket
ALTITUDE: 50m (170ft)
GARDENERS: four

SPECIAL FEATURES: topiary, parterres, herbs, statuary, orangery, Italian garden, Dutch garden, spring wild flowers and daffodils in pleasure grounds

Formal 17th-century gardens by London and Wise to east and north swept away in mid 18th century under the influence of Capability Brown's 'naturalising' school abetted by a devastating flood from former canal to east of house. Small canal to north-east of house now the only surviving 17th-century feature of gardens. 'Italian' garden formed early in 19th century by 1st Earl Brownlow. 1820 orangery by Wyatville. Further embellishments and bedding towards end of 19th century. 'Dutch' garden laid out by 3rd Earl *c.*1880, a replica in part of the earlier London and Wise parterre, in consciously 17th-century style to harmonise with north front of house. Mid 18th-century wilderness to west of house planted with specimen trees in 19th century. 18th- and 19th-century pleasure grounds to north and east in the process of restoration.

BEST TIMES TO VISIT: All year round. Spring for wild flowers and daffodils in pleasure grounds
SEASON: April to end October
PUBLICATIONS: Section in Book of the House
ROUTES: Paths throughout garden. Lakeside walk
FACILITIES: Restaurant, WCs, shop
FACILITIES FOR DISABLED VISITORS: Wheelchair access. Guide dogs admitted. Textured tree bark. ♿ WC
LOCATION: 3m NE of Grantham on A607, signposted from A1 [130:SK929395]
OTHER GARDENS IN AREA: Belvoir Castle (not NT), Fulbeck Castle (not NT)

Blickling Hall

Blickling, Norwich, Norfolk NR11 6NF
Tel: Aylsham (01263) 733084

SOIL & TERRAIN: lime-free soil. Level terrain
ALTITUDE: 30m (100ft)
GARDENERS: six
SPECIAL FEATURES: sunken garden, wilderness garden

Delightful garden and park surrounding magnificent Jacobean house. Victorian sunken garden, remodelled by Norah Lindsay in the 1930s, consisting of four colourful herbaceous beds and yew topiary around a 17th-century fountain. Formal wilderness garden with radial walks lined by avenues of Turkey oak, lime and beech. The northern wilderness area hides a charming secret garden with summerhouse, sundial and scented plants. Late 18th-century orangery, on border of park and garden, houses oranges as well as camellias and ferns. Beyond the garden lies the wooded 18th-century landscape park planted with oak, beech and sweet chestnuts and featuring a long man-made lake.

BEST TIMES TO VISIT: Spring for bluebells in wilderness garden. Summer for colour of herbaceous beds
SEASON: April to end October
PUBLICATIONS: Section in Book of the House and leaflets detailing garden and park walks
ROUTES: Paths around formal areas near house and through wilderness garden. Many good walks in parkland
PLANT SALES: Extensive plant centre open all year round in orchard. Different collections based on plants grown at Blickling, such as the Moat Collection and the Parterre Collection
FACILITIES: Restaurant, shop, Buckinghamshire Arms Inn (B&B), WCs
FACILITIES FOR DISABLED VISITORS: Wheelchair access to grounds. Guide dogs admitted. ♿ WC. Motorised buggy available
LOCATION: On N side of B1354, 1½m NW of Aylsham on A140 [133:TG178286]
OTHER GARDENS IN AREA: Felbrigg Hall, Sheringham Park, Corpusty Mill Gardens (not NT)

Felbrigg Hall

Norwich, Norfolk NR11 8PR Tel: West Runton (01263) 837444

SOIL & TERRAIN: lime-free soil. Level terrain
ALTITUDE: 60.9m (200ft)
GARDENERS: two
SPECIAL FEATURES: NCCPG National Collection of colchicums

Delightful walled garden of 17th-century house combining productive and ornamental gardening. Espaliered fruit trees, vines and figs trained on the walls while beds contain dahlias, roses and herbaceous plantings as well as herbs. Ornamental pond surrounded by a circle of lavender 'Hidcote' which proves popular with bees from the hives in the apple orchard. Colchicums (NCCPG National Collection) line the shrub borders and provide spectacular autumn display. Octagonal dovecote with fantail doves. Formal grounds around hall with orangery and arboretum. In addition to garden there are acres of undulating parkland with mature woodland of maples, sycamores, oaks and beeches and a lake.

BEST TIMES TO VISIT: Spring for blossom. Summer for roses and border displays. Autumn for fruit and autumn crocuses. Parkland good all year
SEASON: March to end October. Parkland open all year
PUBLICATIONS: Section in property guide. *Felbrigg: The Story of a House* by R.W. Ketton-Cremer (National Trust/Century Classics)
ROUTES: Gravel paths around garden. Free wandering throughout park
FACILITIES: Restaurant, shop, WC
FACILITIES FOR DISABLED VISITORS: ♿ WC. Motorised buggy available. Guide dogs admitted. Scented lavender in walled garden. Braille guide
LOCATION: Nr Felbrigg village, 2m SW of Cromer, entrance off B1436 [133:TG193394]
OTHER GARDENS IN AREA: Blickling Hall, Sheringham Park

Gunby Hall

Gunby, nr Spilsby, Lincolnshire PE23 5SS Tel: (01909) 486411

SOIL & TERRAIN: alkaline, variable soil. Level terrain at edge of wolds. Exposed to severe winds from NE off sea in winter

ALTITUDE: 30m (100ft)
GARDENERS: two

Red-brick, walled 17th-century gardens with contemporary dovecote. Arched pergolas of fruit trees; herbaceous and cutting borders; roses and a herb garden in generous profusion. Kitchen garden with old-fashioned mixture of vegetables, fruit and flowers. Lawns to the east of the house extend to a wild garden and shrubbery. Much planting early in 19th century by Peregrine Massingberd (including a massive cedar of Lebanon in 1812) and again in early 20th century by Margaret Massingberd. Formal planting of yews as bowling alleys to west of the house date from *c.*1900.

BEST TIMES TO VISIT: All through season something of interest. Late June for roses at their best
SEASON: April to end September
ROUTES: Free wandering
PLANT SALES: Small-scale plant sales
FACILITIES: WCs
FACILITIES FOR DISABLED VISITORS: Wheelchair access to most parts of garden. Guide dogs admitted. Scented plants especially in herb garden
LOCATION: 2½m NW of Burgh-le-Marsh, 7m W of Skegness on S side of A158 [122:TF467668]
OTHER GARDENS IN AREA: Belton House, Burghley House (not NT)

Ickworth

The Rotunda, Horringer, Bury St Edmunds, Suffolk IP29 5QE
Tel: Bury St Edmunds (01284) 735270

SOIL & TERRAIN: limy soil. Exposed site
ALTITUDE: 75m (250ft)
GARDENERS: three
SPECIAL FEATURES: rare trees, Silver Garden. NCCPG National Collection of box

The grounds of Ickworth were designed to reflect the Italianate nature of the remarkable late 18th-century house commissioned by Frederick Augustus Hervey, the extraordinary 4th Earl of Bristol. Heavily wooded garden with yews, evergreen oak and box and paths giving vistas of the house's central rotunda from various points. Garden includes some uncommon trees including a *Koelreuteria paniculata* from North China. The Silver Garden, hidden among the trees, boasts a collection of hexagonal stones poached from the Giant's Causeway. Edwardian-style border planted with boldly coloured flowers fronts the east wing. Terrace walk to the rear of house. Conservatory in the west wing houses potted plants including *Fatshedera lizei* and *Fatsia japonica*. The park surrounding the house contains some of the best examples of ancient specimen trees including oak, beech and hornbeam.

BEST TIMES TO VISIT: Spring for bluebells in Silver Garden. All year round for parkland
SEASON: April to end October
PUBLICATIONS: Garden leaflet with recommended routes. Also section and plan in property guidebook. *The Mitred Earl* by Brian Fothergill (National Trust/Century Classics)
ROUTES: Free wandering in grounds. Several recommended walks through grounds: the Albana Walk, Oak Tree Walk and Lord William Hervey's Walk
FACILITIES: Tea-room, shop, WCs
FACILITIES FOR DISABLED VISITORS: Much of garden accessible to wheelchair users but there are gravel paths. ♿WC
LOCATION: In Horringer, 3m SW of Bury St Edmunds on W side of A143 [155:TL8161]
OTHER GARDENS IN AREA: Melford Hall, Anglesey Abbey

Melford Hall

Long Melford, Sudbury, Suffolk CO10 9AH
Tel: Sudbury (01787) 880286

SOIL & TERRAIN: limy soil. Flat, exposed terrain
ALTITUDE: 30m (100ft)
GARDENERS: one
SPECIAL FEATURES: specimen trees and topiary

Turreted Tudor mansion, originally moated. Garden with lawns planted with specimen trees including a Judas tree, tree of heaven, black mulberry, copper beech and a *Xanthoceras sorbifolium* from the East. Clipped box hedges and topiary. Herbaceous borders planted to original Victorian and Edwardian designs. North arm of moat now planted as a sunken garden.

BEST TIMES TO VISIT: Summer for garden colour
SEASON: April to end October
PUBLICATIONS: Section in property guidebook
ROUTES: Free wandering throughout garden
FACILITIES: Refreshments in Long Melford. WCs
FACILITIES FOR DISABLED VISITORS: Some steps in garden but generally accessible to wheelchair users. ♿WC
LOCATION: In Long Melford on E side of A134, 14m S of Bury St Edmunds [155:TL867462]
OTHER GARDENS IN AREA: Ickworth, Kentwell (not NT)

Oxburgh Hall

Oxborough, nr King's Lynn, Norfolk PE33 9PS
Tel: Gooderstone (0136 621) 258

SOIL & TERRAIN: limy soil. Level terrain
ALTITUDE: 30m (100ft)
GARDENERS: three
SPECIAL FEATURES: parterre. Kitchen garden

Moated house built in 1482 by the Bedingfeld family. Lawns fringed with fine trees. Victorian parterre planted by Sir Henry Paston-Bedingfield in mid 19th century, lined with box and some with permanent plantings of *Cineraria* 'Silver Dust' and *Ruta graveolens* 'Jackman's Blue'. Summer bedding for the parterre includes ageratums and French marigolds. Victorian kitchen garden now planted as formal orchard with plums, medlars, quinces and gages while roses, clematis and other climbers grow on the walls. Long herbaceous border behind yew hedge.

BEST TIMES TO VISIT: Summer for parterre in bloom
SEASON: April to end October
PUBLICATIONS: Section in property guidebook
ROUTES: Free wandering around garden. Good walks in surrounding woodland
FACILITIES: Restaurants, shop, WCs
FACILITIES FOR DISABLED VISITORS: Garden level and accessible for wheelchairs. ♿WC
LOCATION: At Oxborough, 7m SW of Swaffham on S side of Stoke Ferry road [143:TF742012]

Peckover House

North Brink, Wisbech, Cambridgeshire PE13 1JR
Tel: Wisbech (01945) 583463

SOIL & TERRAIN: rich alluvial soil. Level terrain
ALTITUDE: 30m (100ft)
GARDENERS: three
SPECIAL FEATURES: Victorian fernery and orangery

Charming 2-acre Victorian garden of Georgian house originally owned by Quaker banking family. Spacious lawn shaded by specimen trees including a gingko and tulip tree, Chusan palm and monkey puzzle tree. Eastern edge of garden planted with laurels, hollies, box and yew forming a wilderness area. Colourful border planting. Orangery still contains fruit-bearing trees including specimen over 200 years old; also many colourful pot plants. Clematis, honeysuckle and roses ramble over metal arches and brick dividing walls. Elegant summerhouses. Victorian fernery housing many examples of unusual ferns including *Platycerium bifurcatum*, elkhorn fern and hare's foot fern. Greenhouse contains examples of Malmaison carnations.

BEST TIMES TO VISIT: Spring for daffodils, narcissi and wild flowers. Summer for colourful borders
SEASON: April to end October
ROUTES: Free wandering throughout garden
FACILITIES: Teas, WC
FACILITIES FOR DISABLED VISITORS: Garden accessible to wheelchair users, prior notice required. Guide dogs admitted. Scented flowers
LOCATION: On N bank of River Nene in Wisbech (B1441) [143:TF458097]
OTHER GARDENS IN AREA: Sandringham House (not NT)

Wimpole Hall

Arrington, Royston, Hertfordshire SG8 0BW
Tel: Cambridge (01223) 207257

SOIL & TERRAIN: limy soil. Level terrain
ALTITUDE: 30m (100ft)
GARDENERS: two

Twenty-acre garden with 350-acre park beyond. Once an intricate and extensive 17th-century formal garden but has undergone several phases of landscape and garden design since then. Park landscaped by Bridgeman, Capability Brown and Repton and contains folly and Chinese bridge; also $2\frac{1}{4}$-mile avenue, originally of elms which were destroyed by Dutch elm disease, now replanted with limes. Formal garden surrounding the house, which dates from mid 17th century. Enclosed by iron railings it includes an informal rose garden recently created on the site of the Victorian conservatory, planted with roses including 'Nevada', 'Penelope' and 'Fritz Nobis'; a Dutch garden and a restored parterre. 19th-century pleasure grounds to the east of house contain fine specimens of conifers including Bishop's Pine, Spanish fir and Sequoias. This area is underplanted with over 20 varieties of daffodils and narcissi such as 'King Alfred', 'Fortune' and 'Sempre Avanti', and in addition provides an impressive display of wild flowers including snowdrops, celandines, orchids and violets.

BEST TIMES TO VISIT: Spring for daffodils, narcissi and wild flowers. Early summer for roses. Summer for bedding display in parterre
SEASON: April to end October
PUBLICATIONS: Section in Book of the House
ROUTES: Paths throughout garden. Many parkland routes
FACILITIES: Restaurant, tea-room, shop, WCs
FACILITIES FOR DISABLED VISITORS: Garden accessible to wheelchair users. ♿ WC. Motorised buggy available
LOCATION: 8m SW of Cambridge (A603), 6m N of Royston (A14) [154:TL336510]
OTHER GARDENS IN AREA: Anglesey Abbey, Cambridge University Botanic Garden (not NT), Peckover House

North-West England

CUMBRIA · LANCASHIRE · MERSEYSIDE

Acorn Bank Garden

Temple Sowerby, nr Penrith, Cumbria CA10 1SP
Tel: Kirkby Thore (017683) 61893

SOIL & TERRAIN: heavy alkaline soil. Gently sloping site for walled garden. Steep slope in wild garden

ALTITUDE: 75m (250ft)

GARDENERS: one; volunteers

Walled garden of 1½ acres protected by fine oaks under which grow a vast display of daffodils; contains orchards with variety of apple trees; surrounding the orchards are mixed borders with herbaceous plants, shrubs and roses. Herb garden has the largest collection of culinary and medicinal plants in the north. Greenhouse. Sunken garden with pond and dry stone terraces.

BEST TIMES TO VISIT: April to May for spring bulbs, wild flowers and blossom in orchard and wild garden. Herb garden at its best June to early August. July to September borders in walled garden with roses and clematis. Some autumn colour and late flowers in October but can be spoilt by early frost

SEASON: April to end October

PUBLICATIONS: Acorn Bank Garden Guide and herb list

ROUTES: Free wandering in walled garden. Woodland trails outside walled garden

PLANT SALES: Small-scale selection for sale at most times

FACILITIES: WC, small shop, picnic area

FACILITIES FOR DISABLED VISITORS: Wheelchair access to herb and walled gardens (some gravel paths) and greenhouse but not wild garden. Wheelchair for loan. Resting posts and fairly level path on woodland trails. Guide dogs admitted. Scented plants in herb garden. ♿WC

LOCATION: Just N of Temple Sowerby, 6m E of Penrith on A66 [91:NY612281]
OTHER GARDENS IN AREA: Wordsworth House, Dalemain (not NT)

Hill Top

Near Sawrey, Hawkshead, Ambleside, Cumbria LA22 0LF
Tel: Hawkshead (015394) 36269

SOIL & TERRAIN: acid, light and stony soil. Gently sloping and sheltered site
ALTITUDE: 100m (330ft)
GARDENERS: one part-time
SPECIAL FEATURES: mix of trees, shrubs, herbaceous and annual plants as well as vegetables, fruit and herbs. Inspiration of several of Beatrix Potter's stories

A typical early 20th-century cottage garden at the house formerly owned by writer and artist, Beatrix Potter. Covering approximately ¾ acre, the garden is an informal and tightly packed miscellany of flowers, fruit and vegetables. The garden is illustrated in several of Beatrix Potter's books including *The Tale of Jemima Puddleduck* and *The Tale of Tom Kitten*. With the help of these illustrations and by careful study of contemporary photographs the garden has been restored to look much as it did in Beatrix Potter's day. Plant choice has been restricted to those available in her time and many original garden features remain.

BEST TIMES TO VISIT: Late spring and summer when garden is at its most colourful. Try to avoid weekends and Bank Holidays
SEASON: April to end October
PUBLICATIONS: Colour souvenir guide to property
ROUTES: Free wandering
FACILITIES: WCs, shop
FACILITIES FOR DISABLED VISITORS: Wheelchair access possible for garden but not house. Guide dogs admitted
LOCATION: In village of Near Sawrey 2m SE of Hawkshead [96/97:SD370955]
OTHER GARDENS IN AREA: Sizergh Castle, Brockhole (not NT), Holehird (not NT), Levens Hall (not NT)

Rufford Old Hall

Rufford, nr Ormskirk, Lancashire L40 1SG
Tel: Rufford (01704) 821254

SOIL & TERRAIN: sandy, acid loam. Very flat terrain. Surrounded by mature trees such as sycamore, lime, oak, alder

ALTITUDE: 5m (17ft)
GARDENERS: one; one part-time in season

Very little of the garden's history is known. Present layout is Victorian in concept, the time when most of the existing mature trees were planted. When the NT acquired the Hall in 1936 the garden was overrun with *Rhododendron ponticum*. This has gradually been controlled and hardy hybrid rhododendrons and early and late summer-flowering shrubs have been added and underplanted with drifts of ground cover. Victorian zinc statue of Pan. 19th-century lead statue of infant Bacchus. Topiary of yew squirrels, box spirals, cones and balls.

BEST TIMES TO VISIT: Most colourful in late May and early June when rhododendrons and azaleas are in flower
SEASON: April to end October
PUBLICATIONS: Section in property guidebook
ROUTES: Sandstone paths around the Hall. Two circular walks, one following the beech avenue and meadow, the other taking in the canal and woodland
FACILITIES: Tea-room, WCs and shop
FACILITIES FOR DISABLED VISITORS: Wheelchair access but courtyard bumpy and sandstone paths difficult to negotiate. Guide dogs admitted. Scented roses, honeysuckle, azaleas, viburnums and philadelphus
LOCATION: 7m N of Ormskirk, in village of Rufford on E side of A59 [108:SD463160]
OTHER GARDENS IN AREA: Gawthorpe Hall

Sizergh Castle

nr Kendal, Cumbria LA8 8AE Tel: Sedgwick (015395) 60070/60496

SOIL & TERRAIN: light, alkaline soil. Undulating terrain. Sheltered from W winds
ALTITUDE: 60.9m (200ft)
GARDENERS: two
SPECIAL FEATURES: rock garden. NCCPG National Collection of ferns

Main horticultural attraction is the Westmorland stone rock garden, with Japanese maples and dwarf conifers planted in 1926 when the rock garden was built and now of impressive size. Streams and rocky pools display moisture-loving plants, including the fern collection, of which some 200 species and cultivars are grown (part of this is the NCCPG National Collection). Elsewhere in the garden grow shrubs and climbers, some tender on a south-facing wall. In the rose garden species roses are underplanted with ground cover and bulbs. A good herbaceous border gives colour throughout the season with autumn colour a speciality in September. Wild flower garden.

BEST TIMES TO VISIT: All season for fern collection and herbaceous border. April to May for spring flowers. Summer for rose garden. Autumn colour
SEASON: April to end October
PUBLICATIONS: Garden plan. Section in property guidebook
ROUTES: Free wandering throughout garden except over wild flower areas
FACILITIES: Tea-room, shop, WCs
FACILITIES FOR DISABLED VISITORS: Most of garden accessible to wheelchair users (gravel paths). Guide dogs admitted
LOCATION: 3½m S of Kendal [97:SD498878]
OTHER GARDENS IN AREA: Hill Top, Acorn Bank Garden, Levens Hall (not NT), Holker Hall (not NT)

Speke Hall

The Walk, Liverpool, Merseyside L24 1XD Tel: (0151) 427 7231

SOIL & TERRAIN: acid, light soil. Flat terrain. Exposed site but mild climate

ALTITUDE: 30m (100ft)

GARDENERS: three; one trainee

The garden was redesigned between 1855 and 1865 for Richard Watt. The present layout comprises lawns, borders, paths and hedges together with a dry moat. A rose garden, laid out in 1984 and planted with a mixture of shrub, dwarf and clustered floribunda roses, is now a fine feature on the south side of the half-timbered hall. A stream garden has recently been replanted and there has been extensive bulb planting along the main drive. New paths and borders on south lawn. The walk along the earth bund gives fine views across the Mersey to the Welsh hills beyond.

BEST TIMES TO VISIT: Early spring for bulbs. Late spring for rhododendron and bluebell woods. Summer for rose garden and borders

SEASON: All year

PUBLICATIONS: Section in house guidebook. Plan of garden

ROUTES: Various paths around garden, woods and on the bund

FACILITIES: Tea-room, shop (April to October). WCs all year

FACILITIES FOR DISABLED VISITORS: Wheelchair access. Guide dogs admitted. Some scented plants

LOCATION: On N bank of the Mersey, 8m SE of the centre of Liverpool, 1m S of A561, on W side of Liverpool airport [108:SJ419825]

OTHER GARDENS IN AREA: Croxteth Park (not NT), Ness Garden (not NT), Dunham Massey

North-East England

CLEVELAND · NORTHUMBERLAND · NORTH AND WEST YORKSHIRE

Beningbrough Hall

Shipton-by-Beningbrough, York, North Yorkshire YO6 1DD
Tel: York (01904) 470666

SOIL & TERRAIN: light, alkaline soil. S-facing garden
ALTITUDE: 5m (17ft)
GARDENERS: three

SPECIAL FEATURES: American garden, herbaceous plants and climbers. Potting shed and conservatory

Seven-acre garden surrounded by 370 acres of informal landscape park to the south. 18th-century baroque house is flanked by two small recent formal gardens, both enclosed with yew hedging. To the east there is an American shrub garden, the old walled kitchen garden (now turfed), and herbaceous borders including a narrow but spectacular double border. Well-stocked conservatory, vine house and old potting shed are all open. Pond and river walks close by in the park.

BEST TIMES TO VISIT: June to October for herbaceous border and flowering shrubs
SEASON: April to end October
PUBLICATIONS: Section in Book of the House. Garden leaflet
ROUTES: Paths and free wandering throughout garden. Guided walks available most weekends and Bank Holidays
FACILITIES: Restaurant, WCs, shop, wilderness play area
FACILITIES FOR DISABLED VISITORS: Wheelchair access on level gravel paths. ♿ WC. Guide dogs admitted. Scented plants
LOCATION: 8m NW of York, 2m W of Shipton, 2m SE of Linton-on-Ouse (A19) [105:SE516586]
OTHER GARDENS IN AREA: Nunnington Hall, Newby Hall (not NT), Fountains Abbey and Studley Royal, Castle Howard (not NT)

Cragside House

Rothbury, Morpeth, Northumberland NE65 7PX
Tel: Rothbury (01669) 21267

SOIL & TERRAIN: acid, light soil on steep hillside. Exposed aspect at higher levels of country park. House and rock garden sheltered by conifers
ALTITUDE: 152m (500ft)
GARDENERS: three; plus volunteer and trainee help
SPECIAL FEATURES: North American and other conifers, rhododendron hybrids, lakes, Debdon Burn, garden cascade

Cragside House – built for Lord Armstrong, the Victorian engineer, and the first house to be lit by hydro-electricity – is set in 1,000 acres of wooded grounds dating back to 1870. Magnificent 3-acre rock garden surrounds the house and is currently being replanted with heathers, robust alpines and flowering shrubs. Landscaped grounds filled with pre-1900 hybrid rhododendrons and azaleas, along with large areas of *Rhododendron ponticum* and *R. luteum*. The pinetum contains a fine collection of North American conifers – several of them the largest of their species in the British Isles – and the Debdon Burn, with its series of waterfalls, running close by through a deep gorge. New formal garden, with ferneries and orchard house, is now open to the public: for details see 'New Gardens' section on page 169.

BEST TIMES TO VISIT: End May to June for rhododendrons. All year for conifers
PUBLICATIONS: Section in guidebook to property. Garden leaflet
ROUTES: 6-mile country park drive for walking and driving. Many signposted stone paths radiating from house to various destinations on estate. Energy Circuit (1½m) leads around main points of hydraulic interest. Steep stone steps throughout rock garden to house. Free wandering throughout country park. Dogs should be kept on lead
FACILITIES: Restaurant, shop, WCs
FACILITIES FOR DISABLED VISITORS: Wheelchair access difficult in rock garden. Car parks at various points throughout park to ease access. Guide dogs admitted. Textured tree bark, running water and cascades

LOCATION: 13m SW of Alnwick (B6341) and 15m NW of Morpeth. Entrance at Debdon Gate, 1m N of Rothbury (81:NU073022]

OTHER GARDENS IN AREA: Wallington, Belsay Hall (English Heritage)

East Riddlesden Hall

Bradford Road, Keighley, West Yorkshire BD20 5EL
Tel: Keighley (01535) 607075

SOIL & TERRAIN: slightly acid, light soil. Level site protected by walls and trees

ALTITUDE: 75m (250ft)
GARDENERS: one

Small, attractive walled garden designed by Graham Stuart Thomas in 1972 with herb borders added in 1986 and 1989. Gardens and grounds running down to the River Aire cover 12 acres with a monastic fishpond at the front of the house. Traditional formal garden with modern plants and paths to entice visitors to walk round the garden. Borders provide interest over a long period with careful use of colours and foliage. Quiet retreat with many ideas for the home gardener. Herb borders, mixed borders, pollarded robinias, avenue of fruit trees.

BEST TIMES TO VISIT: June when philadelphus and lonicera fill garden with wonderful scents

SEASON: April to end October

PUBLICATIONS: Section in property guidebook

ROUTES: Free wandering

FACILITIES: Tea-room, WCs, shop, car park

FACILITIES FOR DISABLED VISITORS: Wheelchair access but gravel paths. Guide dogs admitted. Scented herb borders for visually impaired visitors

LOCATION: 1m NE of Keighley [104:SE079421]

OTHER GARDENS IN AREA: Golden Acre Park (not NT), The Hollies (not NT), Parceval Hall Gardens (not NT)

Nostell Priory

Doncaster Road, Nostell, nr Wakefield, West Yorkshire WF4 1QE
Tel: Wakefield (01924) 863892

SOIL & TERRAIN: acid, heavy soil. Slightly undulating land in a sheltered valley site
ALTITUDE: 60.9m (200ft)
GARDENERS: two
SPECIAL FEATURES: rhododendrons, lake, menagerie and cockpit

Shrub and woodland garden centred on an informal lake which dates from at least medieval times. Two designs for the garden, by Joseph Perfect and Stephen Switzer, survive from the 1730s. At least some of Switzer's work was carried out but little remains today. Much 19th-century planting of rhododendrons. West of the lake stands a small gothick building – a menagerie designed by Robert Adam. Nearby is a round cockpit but no traces of original enclosures for animals. Handsome 3-arched bridge of 1761 where Wakefield–Doncaster road crosses the lake.

BEST TIMES TO VISIT: May to June for rhododendrons
SEASON: April to end October
PUBLICATIONS: Section on garden in property guidebook
ROUTES: Paths through garden
FACILITIES: Tea-room in stables (not NT), shop (not NT), WCs
FACILITIES FOR DISABLED VISITORS: Grounds accessible. ♿ WC
LOCATION: On A638 from Wakefield to Doncaster [111:SE407172]
OTHER GARDENS IN AREA: East Riddlesden Hall, Beningbrough Hall, Lotherton Hall (not NT), Yorkshire Sculpture Park (not NT), Bramham Park (not NT)

Nunnington Hall

Nunnington, York, North Yorkshire YO6 5UY
Tel: Nunnington (0143 95) 283

SOIL & TERRAIN: medium loam. Sloping, N-facing site
ALTITUDE: 60m (175ft)
GARDENERS: one

Gardens surrounding delightful 17th-century manor house on the

River Rye. Restoration began during 1980s to reflect various periods in history of house. Terraces, avenues and orchards are typical 17th-century features, whereas the rose garden was introduced in the 1920s by Mrs Fife who gave Nunnington Hall to the NT. Popular sheltered tea-garden on riverside. Orchards feature original varieties of local Ryedale apples and wild meadow flowers. Peacocks in the grounds. Expanding collection of clematis.

BEST TIMES TO VISIT: Spring for flowers and blossom. Garden can become crowded on weekend afternoons in July and August
SEASON: April to end October
PUBLICATIONS: Section in property guidebook
ROUTES: Free wandering
FACILITIES: Tea-room, WCs, shop, baby changing room, tea-garden
FACILITIES FOR DISABLED VISITORS: Wheelchair access to garden. Guide dogs admitted. ♿WC. Scented plants in tea-garden borders
LOCATION: 4½m SE of Helmsley [92:SE670795]
OTHER GARDENS IN AREA: Beningbrough Hall, Ormesby Hall, Treasurer's House, Rievaulx Terrace, Castle Howard (not NT), Duncombe Park (not NT)

Ormesby Hall

Ormesby, Middlesbrough, Cleveland TS7 9AS
Tel: Middlesbrough (01642) 324188

SOIL & TERRAIN: alkaline, heavy soil. Level terrain
ALTITUDE: 46m (155ft)
GARDENERS: one

SPECIAL FEATURES: spring woodland garden, wall shrubs, massed narcissi, species trees, Victorian holly walk, ha-ha

Five-acre garden with a variety of contrasting areas. Formal rosebeds to the west and south. Wall shrubs – roses, wisteria, honeysuckle, clematis – clothe the walls of the 18th-century mansion. Borders of mixed planting. Delightful spring woodland garden with wild flowers. Massed daffodils, narcissi, cowslips and frittillaria. Victorian holly walk. Specimen trees and shrubs, and azalea bed. Croquet lawn in regular use.

BEST TIMES TO VISIT: Opening of season in April to May with spring bulbs. June onwards for roses and flowering shrubs. September to October for autumn colours
SEASON: April to October
FACILITIES: Tea-room, shop, WCs, croquet
FACILITIES FOR DISABLED VISITORS: Wheelchair access on gravel paths and lawns. Guide dogs admitted. Scented shrubs, roses and pine trees
LOCATION: On B1380 in Ormesby village, 3m SE of Middlesbrough [93:NZ530167]
OTHER GARDENS IN AREA: Middlesbrough Botanic Garden (not NT), Rievaulx Terrace, Duncombe Park (not NT), Nunnington Hall

Rievaulx Terrace and Temples

Rievaulx, Helmsley, North Yorkshire YO6 5LJ
Tel: Bilsdale (0143 96) 340

SOIL & TERRAIN: alkaline, light soil. Level plateau falling steeply to the W. Exposed
ALTITUDE: 180m (550ft)
GARDENERS: one

SPECIAL FEATURES: fine 18th-century landscape garden. Ionic and Tuscan Temples. Views to Rievaulx Abbey (English Heritage). Lawns with native and broadleaved woodlands. Dramatic location and landscape views

Mid 18th-century landscape terrace garden overlooking deeply incised valley of the River Rye. Laid out in 1758 by Thomas Duncombe III. Serpentine terrace with its two temples (Tuscan and Ionic) – one at each end – contrasts with the formality of the Duncombe Terrace at nearby Duncombe Park, Helmsley. Outstanding example of picturesque informal taste in English landscape gardening. Lawned terrace ½ mile in length is framed by backdrop woodland of beech, ash and variegated sycamore. Low shrub border of alpine currant, mock orange, lilac and snowberry fringes the terrace. Woodland below terrace designated a Site of Special Scientific Interest for its native broadleaved tree, shrub and plant communities. Terrace bank managed for wild flowers such as cowslips, primroses, orchids, violets and ladies bedstraw.

BEST TIMES TO VISIT: Throughout season. If possible avoid Bank Holidays and weekends in July and August
SEASON: April to end October
PUBLICATIONS: Booklet. Also fold-out leaflet with plan *An Introduction to Rievaulx Terrace & Temples*
ROUTES: Marked routes and free wandering. Woodland walk recommended, returning along the terrace
FACILITIES: Information room, shop, WCs
FACILITIES FOR DISABLED VISITORS: Motorised buggy available. Guide dogs admitted. No access for wheelchairs to temples
LOCATION: 2½m NW of Helmsley on B1257 (Stokesley road) [100:SE579848]
OTHER GARDENS IN AREA: Nunnington Hall, Duncombe Park (not NT), Ormesby Hall, Castle Howard (not NT), Sutton Park (not NT), Newburgh Priory (not NT)

Studley Royal

Fountains, Ripon, North Yorkshire HG4 3DY
Tel: Ripon (01765) 608888

SOIL & TERRAIN: brown earth overlying limestone and gritstone. Sheltered site in valley of River Skell
ALTITUDE: 100m (330ft)
GARDENERS: six

SPECIAL FEATURES: formal water features, lawns, trees, garden buildings, statuary and vistas. Georgian 'green' garden little altered since its inception

Superb water garden of 150 acres created by John Aislabie in the 18th century. Now the least altered Georgian 'green' garden in England, characterised by mirror-like stretches of water in which garden buildings and other features are reflected, set in lawns bordered by yew hedges and surrounded by plantations of forest trees, many evergreen. The landscape incorporates the ruins of Fountains Abbey, the Jacobean Fountains Hall and a 400-acre deer park where W. Burges's 19th-century church, St Mary's, is situated. The Fountains Abbey and Studley Royal estate was designated a World Heritage Site in 1987.

BEST TIMES TO VISIT: All year round
SEASON: All year
PUBLICATIONS: Souvenir guide to whole property. Garden/park leaflet with bird's-eye view
ROUTES: Paths leading around property and areas of open access
FACILITIES: Visitor centre with exhibition and visual programme, free guided tours of garden in summer, car park, restaurant, tea-room, shop, WCs
FACILITIES FOR DISABLED VISITORS: Wheelchair access to most parts of garden. Powered and manual wheelchairs available. Minibus. Guide dogs admitted. ♿ WC
LOCATION: 4m W of Ripon off B6265, signposted from A1 [99:SE271683]
OTHER GARDENS IN AREA: Beningbrough Hall, Newby Hall (not NT), Harlow Carr Gardens (not NT), Parceval Hall Gardens (not NT)

Wallington

Cambo, Morpeth, Northumberland NE61 4AR
Tel: Scots' Gap (0167074) 283

SOIL & TERRAIN: neutral to acid soil with varying texture. Level terrain with gentle slopes. Sheltered by trees
ALTITUDE: 152m (500ft)
GARDENERS: five

SPECIAL FEATURES: National Collection of *Sambucus*, conservatory, ponds, walled garden and conservatory. Wild garden in east woods. Shrubs and herbaceous borders

Gardens and parkland originate in formal schemes of late 17th century. The owner, Sir Walter Blackett, established present balance of woodland, open meadow and ponds between 1728 and

1777 together with much of the sculpture and buildings. Succeeding generations of the family have added to the gardens, introducing exotic plants and trees. Walled garden created in 1760 – once a vegetable garden but now shelters Wallington's most delicate plants with a conservatory restored in 1988. Garden given to the NT by Sir Charles Trevelyan in 1942.

BEST TIMES TO VISIT: Late spring for flowering shrubs. Summer for herbaceous borders. Tremendous autumn colour in woodlands. Colourful display in conservatory all year round

SEASON: All year

PUBLICATIONS: Garden leaflet. Wansbeck Walks leaflet

ROUTES: Paths through woods, free wandering near house and in walled garden

FACILITIES: Restaurant, shop, WCs

FACILITIES FOR DISABLED VISITORS: Wheelchair access. Motorised buggy. Guide dogs admitted. Some scented plants in walled garden and conservatory. Water features

LOCATION: 12m W of Morpeth (B6343), 6m NW of Belsay (A696), take B6342 to Cambo [81:NZ030843]

OTHER GARDENS IN AREA: Cragside, Belsay Hall (English Heritage)

Northern Ireland

Ardress

Annaghmore, Portadown, Craigavon, Co. Armagh BT62 1SQ
Tel: Annaghmore (01762) 851236

SOIL & TERRAIN: heavy soil. S- and E-sloping exposed site
ALTITUDE: 58m (175ft)
GARDENERS: none
SPECIAL FEATURES: mixed border. Formal rose garden with early Irish types of roses

Farmhouse dating from 17th century. Main front and garden façades added in 18th century by owner/architect George Ensor. Small rectangular formal rose garden planted with varieties of early Irish roses. Display of farm implements and livestock in adjoining farmyard.

BEST TIMES TO VISIT: June to August for roses
SEASON: April to end September
PUBLICATIONS: Section in property guidebook
ROUTES: Marked routes
FACILITIES: WCs, children's play area
FACILITIES FOR DISABLED VISITORS: Wheelchair access. Guide dogs admitted. ♿WC
LOCATION: 7m from Portadown on Moy road (B28), 5m from Moy, 3m from Loughgall intersection 13 on M1, 9m from Armagh [H914559]
OTHER GARDENS IN AREA: The Argory

Castle Ward

Strangford, Downpatrick, Co. Down BT30 7LS
Tel: Strangford (01396) 881204

SOIL & TERRAIN: acid, light soil. Rocky terrain. Sheltered site
ALTITUDE: 24.3m (80ft)
GARDENERS: one; plus trainee
SPECIAL FEATURES: semi-tender plants, lake

The sunken Parterre Garden was created by the Ward family in the 19th century on the site of an earlier 18th-century walled garden. Now features a marble statue of Neptune standing in a circular pool. The borders around the sunken garden contain a remarkable collection of tender perennials and shrubs. A row of Irish yews was pruned to resemble its depiction in a 19th-century painting. Recently the flights of steps constructed with wooden poles were replaced with rustic brick. Above the sunken garden is a Victorian rockery and pinetum. Close to the shores of Strangford Lough is the Temple Water, an early 18th-century canal-shaped lake, one of the few remaining 18th-century landscape features in Ireland. Extensive drystone revetting has been constructed along the banks to prevent wave erosion. 19th-century lime walk planted on site of a second small canal was cleared and replanted in 1984 after many of the original trees had fallen. Behind the 17th-century tower house is a 3-step common yew terrace, dating back to the 18th century. The yews have recently undergone tree surgery and some replanting is planned.

BEST TIMES TO VISIT: June to July for colours. Can be busy at Bank Holidays
SEASON: All year
PUBLICATIONS: Section in guidebook
ROUTES: Free wandering throughout
FACILITIES: Restaurant, tea-room, WCs, shop
FACILITIES FOR DISABLED VISITORS: Wheelchair access. Guide dogs admitted. Scented plants. Textured tree bark. ♿WC
LOCATION: 7m NE of Downpatrick, $1\frac{1}{2}$m W of Strangford village on A25, on S shore of Strangford Lough [J752494]
OTHER GARDENS IN AREA: Mount Stewart, Rowallane Garden, Castlewellan Forest Park (not NT)

Florence Court

Enniskillen, Co. Fermanagh BT92 1DB
Tel: Florencecourt (01365) 348249

SOIL & TERRAIN: heavy, acid soil. Undulating and exposed site
ALTITUDE: 60.9m (200ft)
GARDENERS: one
SPECIAL FEATURES: origin of the Irish yew. Informal shrubs and trees. Views, watermill, walled garden, hydraulic ram and summerhouse

The 600-acre park with the Florence Court demesne, created *c.*1789 by William King for the 1st Earl of Enniskillen, features a serpentine avenue, the white walk (which leads through rolling park and woodland to Florence Court itself). To the south the pleasure ground, created *c.*1840 to the design of James Frazer (1793–1863), is rich in azaleas, rhododendrons and viburnums. The original Irish or Florence Court yew (*Taxus baccata* 'fastigiata') still grows on the estate. Found growing wild in the 1760s, this tree can only be propagated by cuttings. Many old estate features (such as a walled garden, summerhouse, ice house, eel house and bridge) have survived and are gradually being restored. Much new planting has taken place to restore the 18th-century form.

BEST TIMES TO VISIT: Spring for display of daffodils, rhododendrons and azaleas. Summer for roses. Autumn for changing colours
SEASON: April to end September
PUBLICATIONS: Section in guidebook
ROUTES: Marked paths but also free wandering
FACILITIES: Restaurant, WCs, shop, picnic site
FACILITIES FOR DISABLED VISITORS: Wheelchair access to all of garden. Motorised buggy available. Guide dogs admitted
LOCATION: 1m W of Florencecourt village. 8m SW of Enniskillen via A4 and A32 [H175344]
OTHER GARDENS IN AREA: Landscapes at Castle Coole and Crom

Mount Stewart

Newtownards, Co. Down BT22 2AD
Tel: Greyabbey (012477) 88387/88487

SOIL & TERRAIN: acid, light soil. SW-facing site, sloping up from sea level

ALTITUDE: 15m (50ft)
GARDENERS: six

Fascinating 18th-century house where Lord Castlereagh grew up. Garden created by Edith, wife of the 7th Marquess of Londonderry, in the 1920s with an unrivalled collection of plants that thrive in the mild climate of the Ards peninsula. Garden covers 75 to 80 acres and contains colourful parterres, magnificent vistas and views around the 5-acre lake. The Temple of the Winds, James 'Athenian' Stuart's banqueting hall of 1785, overlooks Strangford Lough. Rhododendrons and many exotic trees. Unique collection of trees and shrubs from southern hemisphere. Statuary including Dodo Terrace with figures representing family and friends of Lady Londonderry.

BEST TIMES TO VISIT: May for rhododendrons. Summer for colour in flower beds
SEASON: March to end October
PUBLICATIONS: Garden guidebook
ROUTES: Paths throughout garden. Maps at strategic points
FACILITIES: Restaurant/tea-room, WCs, shop
FACILITIES FOR DISABLED VISITORS: Most of the garden accessible by wheelchair. Guide dogs admitted. Scented plants
LOCATION: 15m E of Belfast on A20 Newtownards–Portaferry road, 5m SE of Newtownards [J553695]
OTHER GARDENS IN AREA: Rowallane Garden, Castle Ward

Rowallane Garden

Saintfield, Ballynahinch, Co. Down BT24 7LH
Tel: Saintfield (01238) 510131

SOIL & TERRAIN: acid soil overlying rock. Undulating terrain with shelter belts
ALTITUDE: 60.9m (200ft)
GARDENERS: five

SPECIAL FEATURES: daffodils and rhododendrons, fuchsias and shrub roses, rock garden with primula, meconopsis, heathers and dwarf shrubs. Areas of wild flowers. Rare collectors' material. NCCPG National Collection of large-flowered penstemons

The Rev. John Moore gradually enlarged his farmhouse during the 19th century, adding the stable block and planting the pleasure grounds. Stone seats and cairns are left by him. In 1903 he bequeathed Rowallane to his nephew, Hugh Armytage Moore, who had a rare gift for planning and a great eye for plants. Very little landscaping has been carried out at Rowallane, resulting in 52 acres of delightful natural garden. Rare specimens of plants, such as the Chilean fire bush and the handkerchief tree sent back from the Far East and southern hemisphere by such collectors as E.H. Wilson, G. Forrest and F. Kingdon-Ward, appear throughout the garden. In 1942 the Royal Horticultural Society awarded Hugh Armytage Moore the Victoria Medal of Honour.

BEST TIMES TO VISIT: Spring display. End April to mid June for rhododendrons and azaleas. Walled gardens in the summer. Rock garden interesting throughout year. October to November for spectacular autumn colours
SEASON: All year
PUBLICATIONS: Garden plan
ROUTES: Free wandering
PLANT SALES: Sale of surplus plants (mostly herbaceous) during Autumn Garden Week (tel. for dates)
FACILITIES: Tea-room, WCs, shops
FACILITIES FOR DISABLED VISITORS: Wheelchair access. ♿ WC. Scented plants

LOCATION: 11m SE of Belfast, 1m S of Saintfield, W of the Downpatrick road (A7) [J412581]
OTHER GARDENS IN AREA: Castle Ward, Mount Stewart

Springhill

Moneymore, Magherafelt, Co. Londonderry BT45 7NQ
Tel: Moneymore (0164 87) 48210

SOIL & TERRAIN: acid, light soil. Level terrain
ALTITUDE: 30m (100ft)
GARDENERS: one
SPECIAL FEATURES: small walled gardens. Herbs. Groups of ancient yews planted in 18th century

'Planter' house from 17th century with 18th- and 19th-century additions. Home of 10 generations of the Lenox Conyngham family. Set in 45 acres of grounds with various small walled gardens containing a mixture of old roses and herbaceous plants. Herbs and other culinary plants are well represented. Also a 'camomile lawn' in the herb garden.

BEST TIMES TO VISIT: Spring and summer for roses and border colour
SEASON: April to end September
PUBLICATIONS: Section in property guidebook
ROUTES: Free wandering throughout garden
FACILITIES: Tea-room, WCs
FACILITIES FOR DISABLED VISITORS: Wheelchair access. Guide dogs admitted. Herb garden. ♿ WC
LOCATION: 1m from Moneymore on Moneymore–Coagh road (B18) [H866828]
OTHER GARDENS IN AREA: Ardress

South-West England

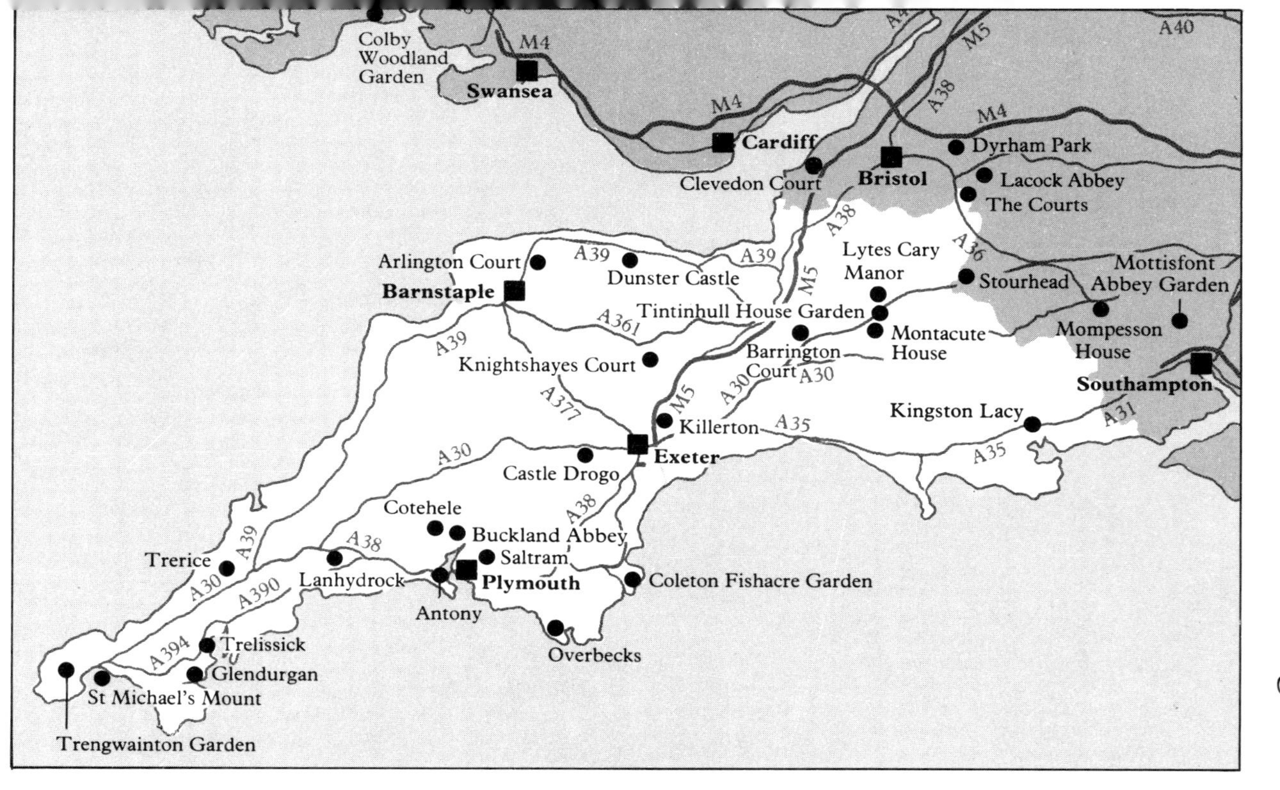

Southern England

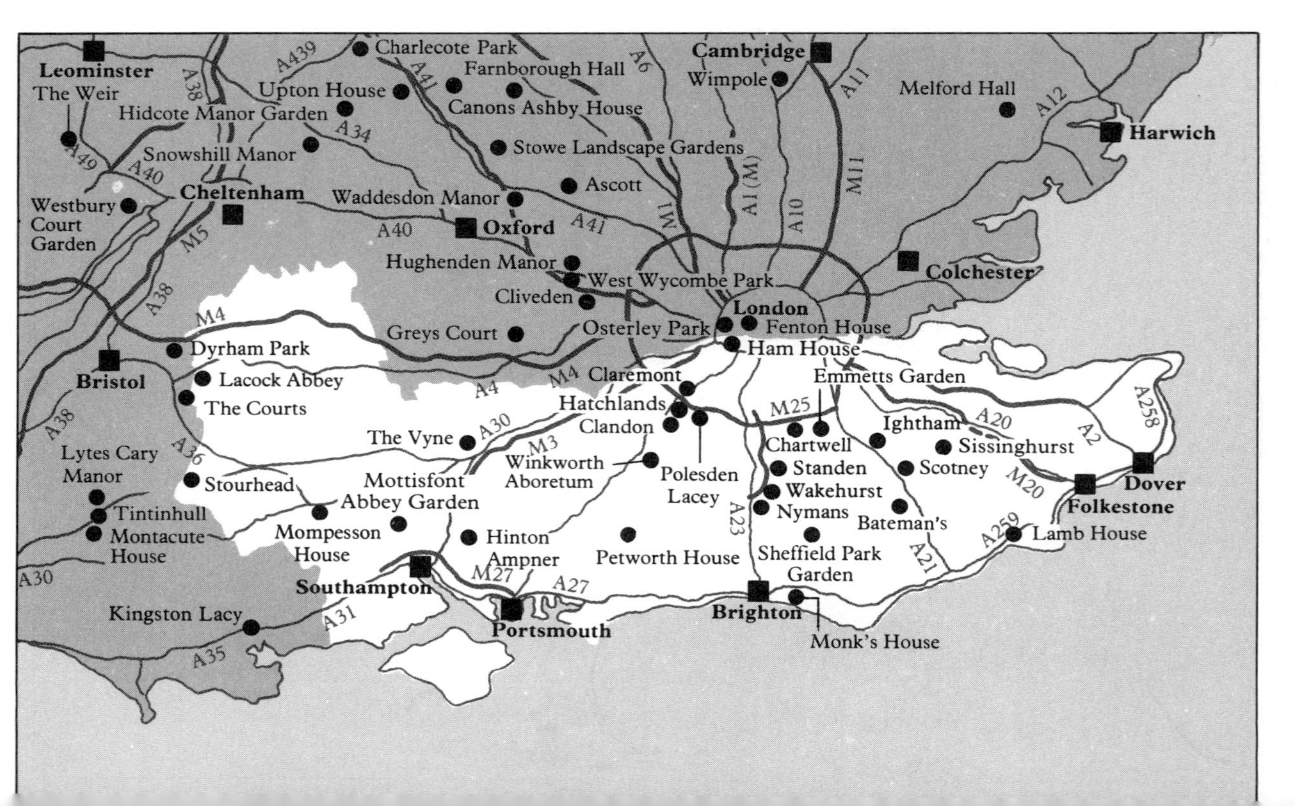

Wales and the Welsh Borders

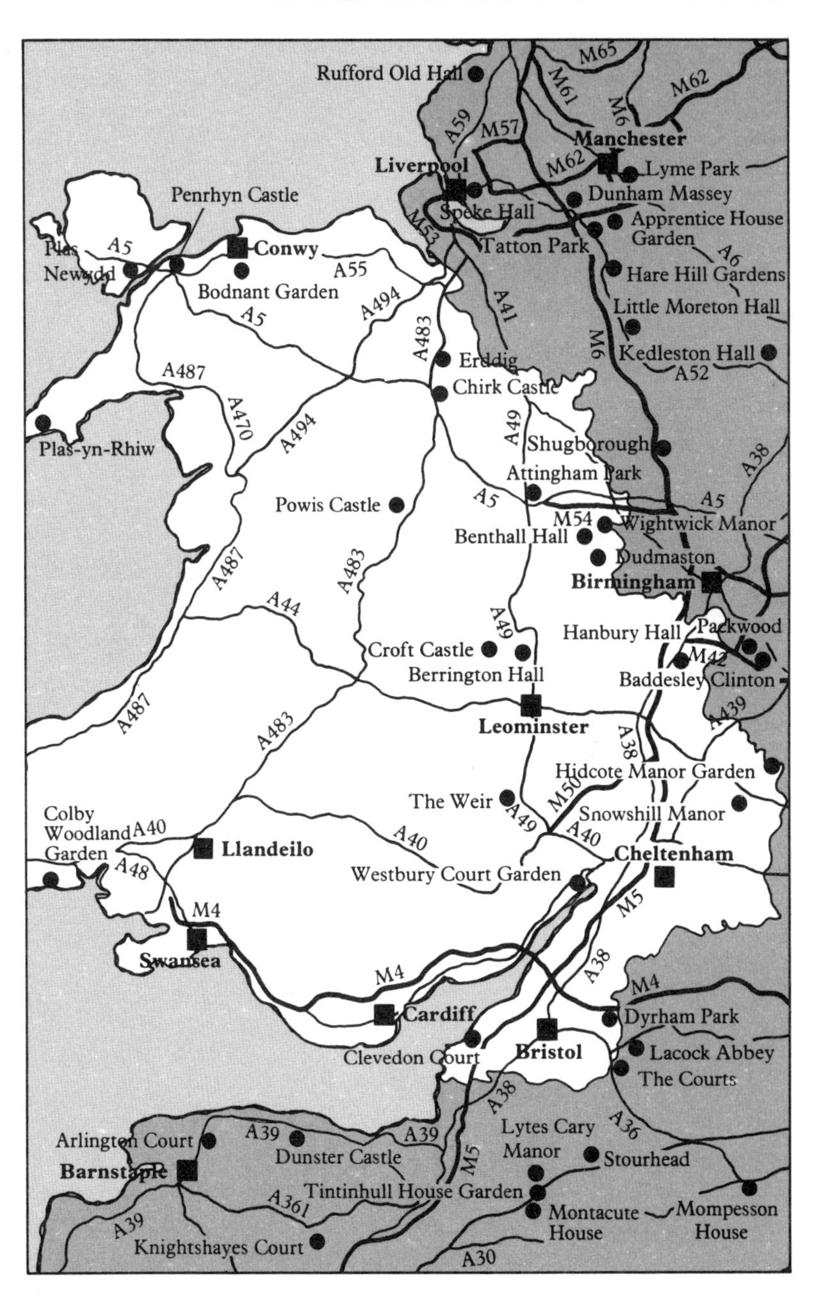

London, Thames Valley and the Chilterns

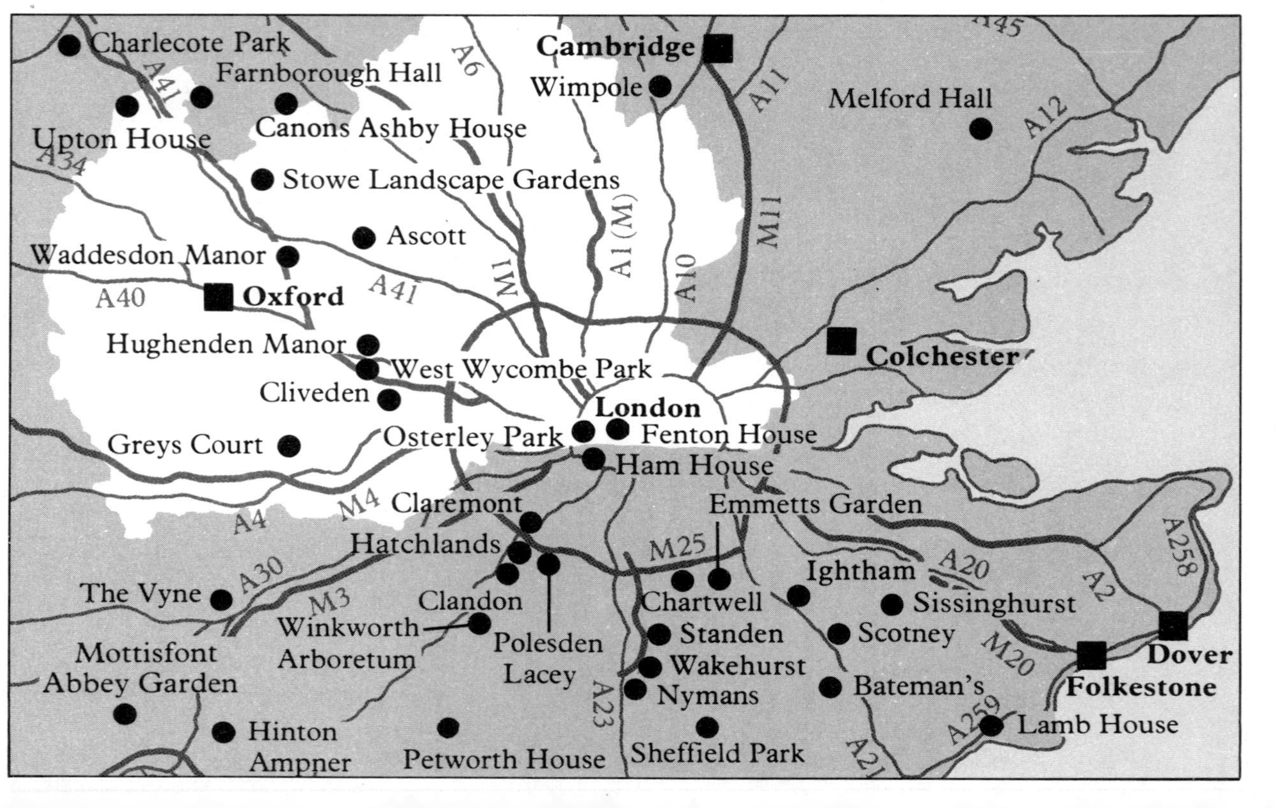

Heart of England

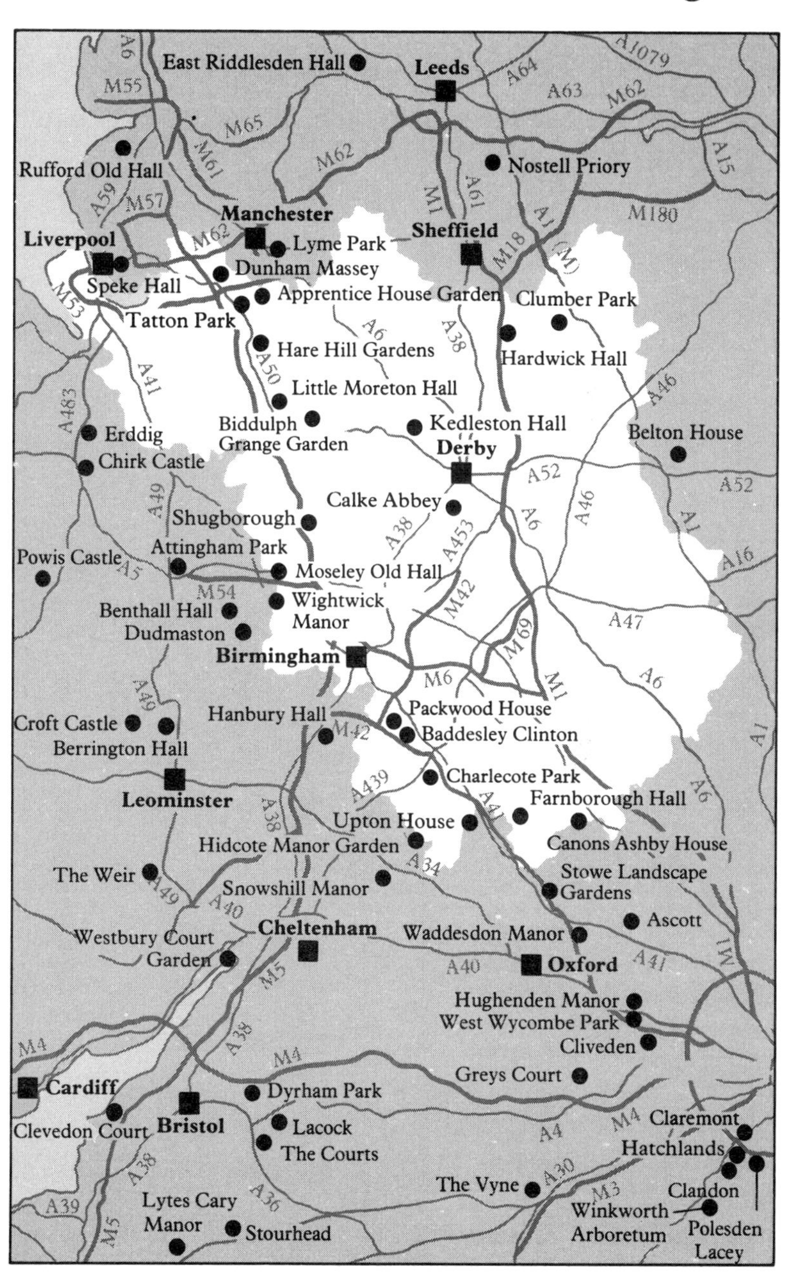

Eastern Counties

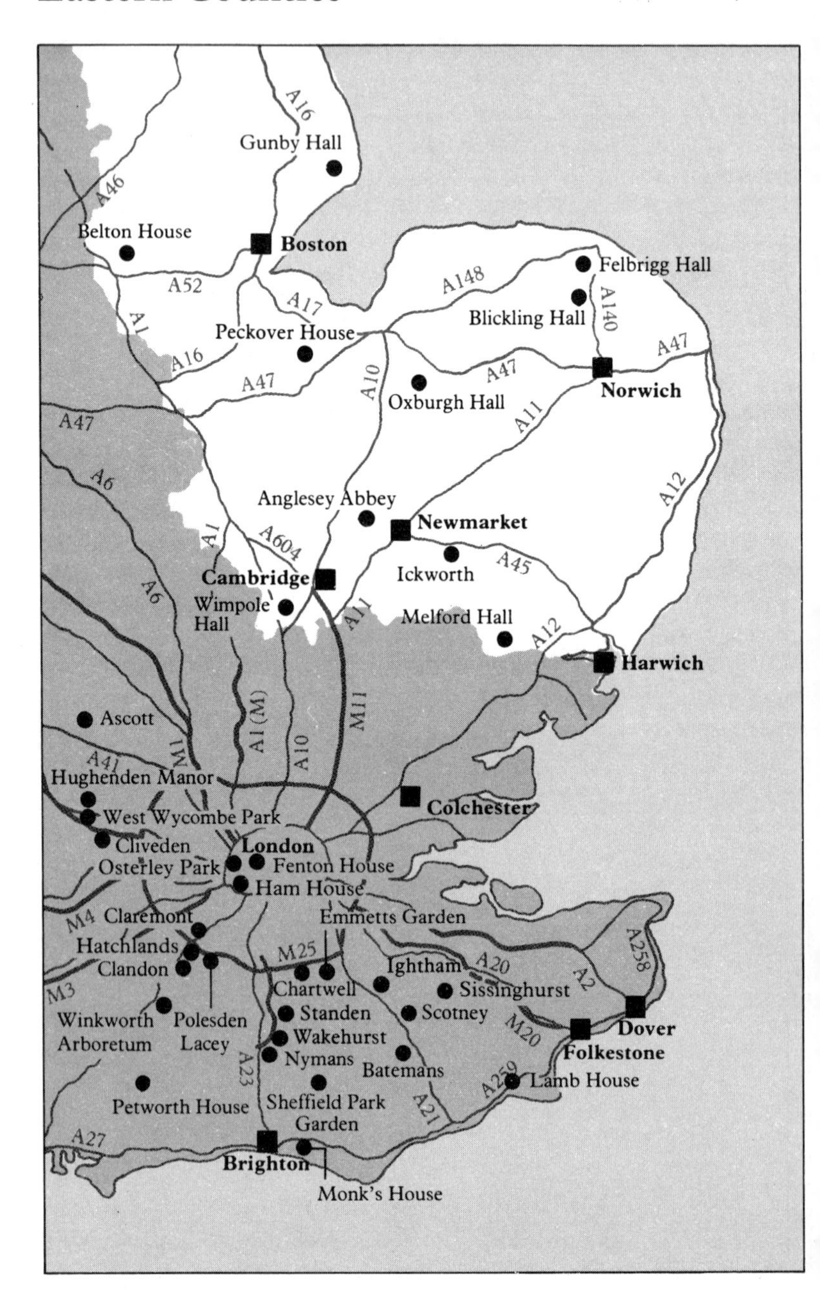

North-West and North-East England

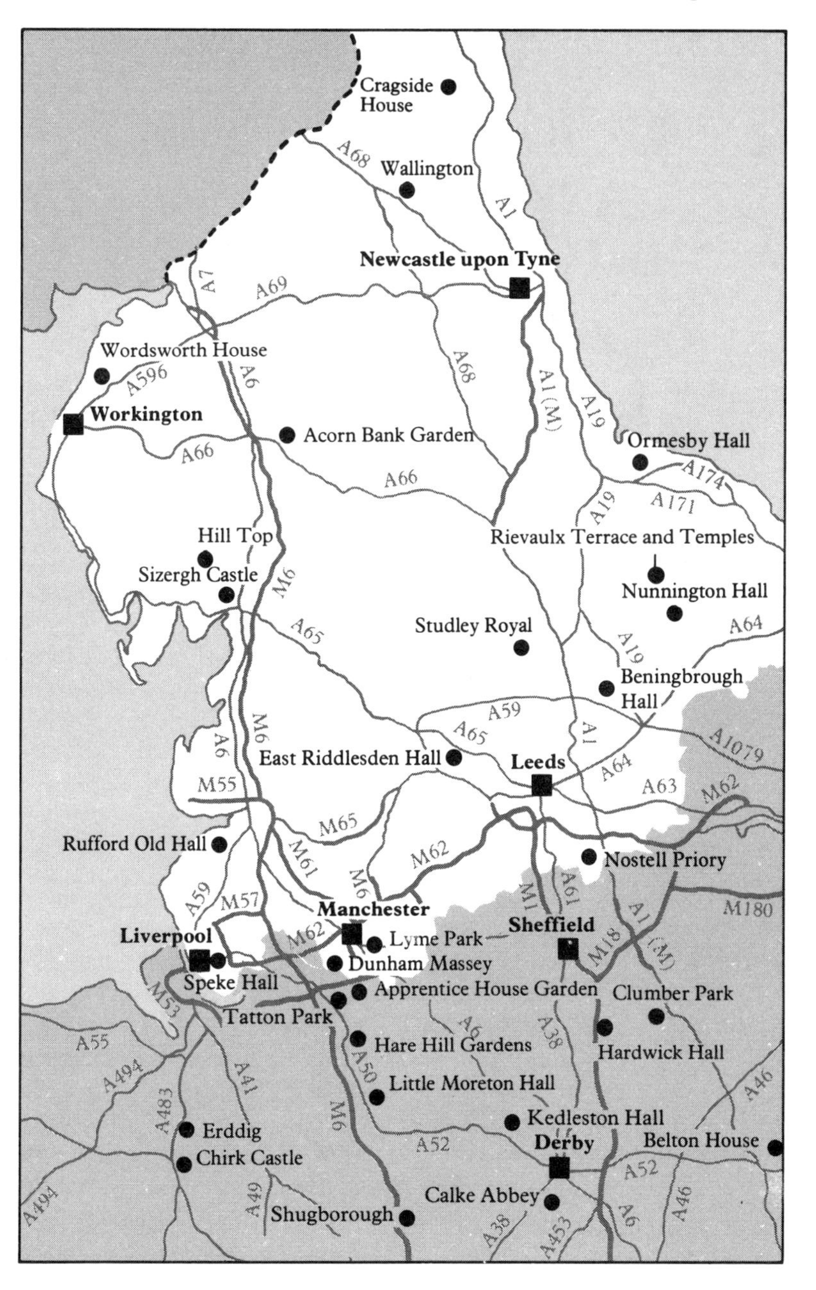

Northern Ireland

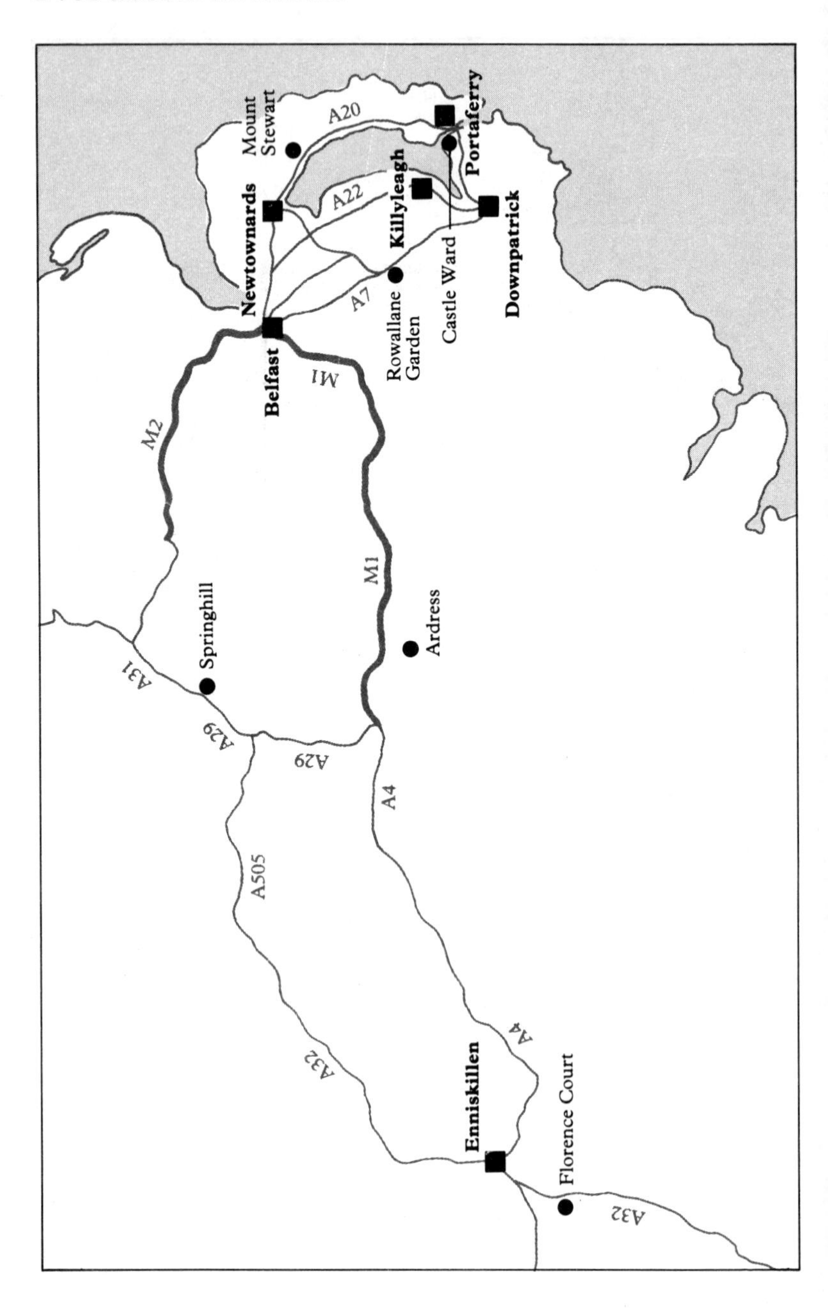

INFORMATION

Regional Offices

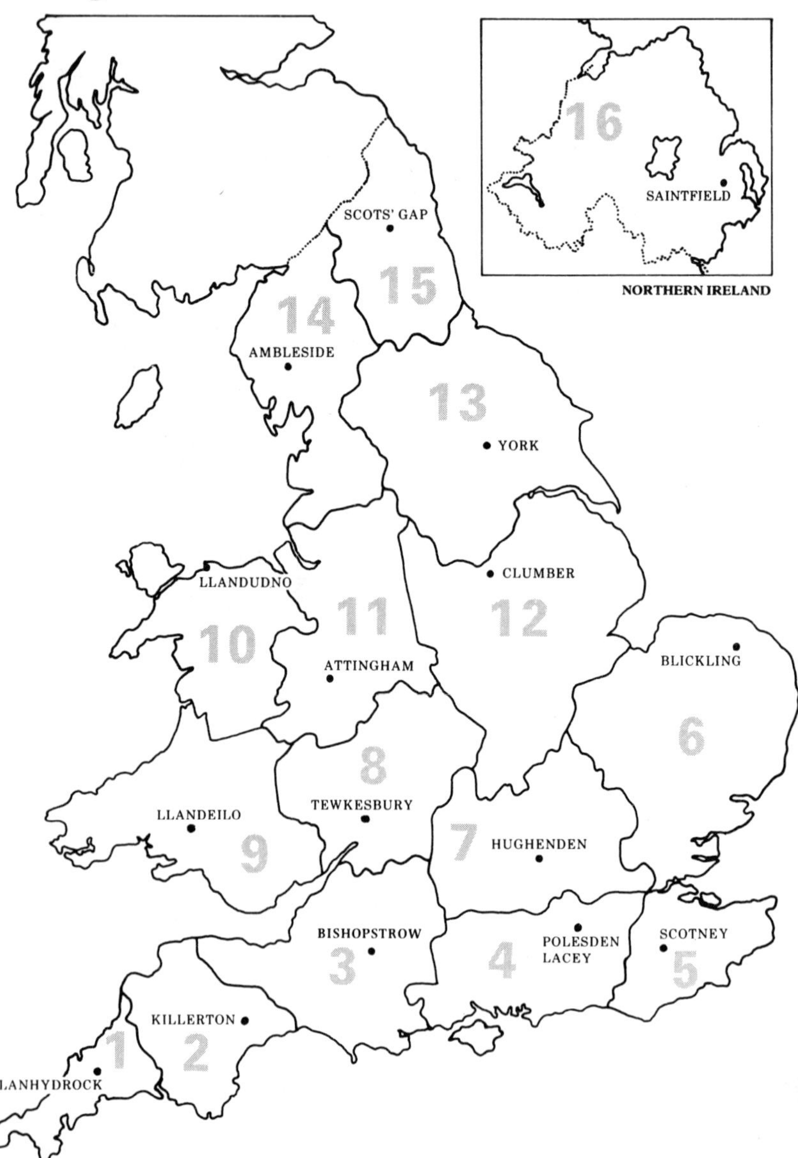

Useful Addresses

London Office: 36 Queen Anne's Gate, London SW1H 9AS (0171-222 9251)
London Information Centre: Blewcoat School, 23 Caxton Street, London SW1H 0PY (0171-222 2877)
Membership: PO Box 39, Bromley, Kent BR1 3XL (0181-464 1111)
Finance; Internal Audit: Heywood House, Westbury, Wiltshire BA13 4NA (Westbury (01373) 826826)
Enterprises: The Stable Block, Heywood House (as above) (Westbury (01373) 858787)

1 **Cornwall:** Lanhydrock, Bodmin PL30 4DE (Bodmin (01208) 74281)

2 **Devon:** Killerton House, Broadclyst, Exeter EX5 3LE (Exeter (01392) 881691)

3 **Wessex** (*Avon, Dorset, Somerset, Wiltshire*) Eastleigh Court, Bishopstrow, Warminster, Wiltshire BA12 9HW (Warminster (01985) 847777)

4 **Southern** (*Hampshire, Isle of Wight, South-Western Greater London, Surrey and West Sussex*) Polesden Lacey, Dorking, Surrey RH5 6BD (Bookham (01372) 453401)

5 **Kent & East Sussex** (*includes South-Eastern Greater London*) The Estate Office, Scotney Castle, Lamberhurst, Tunbridge Wells, Kent TN3 8JN (Lamberhurst (01892) 890651)

6 **East Anglia** (*Cambridgeshire, Essex, Norfolk, Suffolk*) Blickling, Norwich NR11 6NF (Aylsham (01263) 733471)

7 **Thames & Chilterns** (*Buckinghamshire, Bedfordshire, Berkshire, Hertfordshire, London north of the Thames, and Oxfordshire*) Hughenden Manor, High Wycombe, Bucks HP14 4LA (High Wycombe (01494) 528051)

8 **Severn** (*Gloucestershire, Hereford & Worcester, Warwickshire, part of West Midlands*) Mythe End House, Tewkesbury, Glos GL20 6EB (Tewkesbury (01684) 850051)

9 **South Wales** (*Dyfed, Gwent, West Glamorgan, southern part of Powys*) The King's Head, Bridge Street, Llandeilo, Dyfed SA19 6BN (Llandeilo (01558) 822800)

10 **North Wales** (*Clwyd, Gwynedd, northern part of Powys*) Trinity Square, Llandudno, Gwynedd LL30 2DE (Llandudno (01492) 860123)

11 **Mercia** (*Cheshire, Merseyside, Shropshire, Greater Manchester, most of Staffordshire, part of West Midlands*) Attingham Park, Shrewsbury, Shropshire SY4 4TP (Upton Magna (01743) 709343)

12 **East Midlands** (*Derbyshire, Leicestershire, Lincolnshire, Northamptonshire, Nottinghamshire, South Humberside and parts of Cheshire, Greater Manchester, Staffordshire, South Yorkshire and West Yorkshire*) Clumber Park Stableyard, Worksop, Notts S80 3BE (Worksop (01909) 486411)

13 **Yorkshire** (*includes North, South and West Yorkshire, Cleveland and North Humberside*) Goddards, 27 Tadcaster Road, Dringhouses, York YO2 2QG (York (01904) 702021)

14 **North-West** (*Cumbria and Lancashire*) The Hollens, Grasmere, Ambleside, Cumbria LA22 9QZ (Ambleside (015394) 35599)

15 **Northumbria** (*Durham, Northumberland and Tyne & Wear*) Scots' Gap, Morpeth, Northumberland NE61 4EG (Scots' Gap (0167 074) 691)

16 **Northern Ireland:** Rowallane House, Saintfield, Ballynahinch, Co. Down BT24 7LH (Saintfield (01238) 510721)

A Calendar for Visiting

November to March

BODNANT	*daffodils and early magnolias*
KILLERTON	*spring flowers, magnolias*
KINGSTON LACY	*snowdrops*
LANHYDROCK	*magnolias and camellias*
OVERBECKS	*rare and tender shrubs, magnolias*
POLESDEN LACEY	*winter-flowering plants*
STOURHEAD	*trees, conifers, landscape, Lent lilies*
STUDLEY ROYAL & FOUNTAINS ABBEY	*water garden and landscape*
THE WEIR	*very early spring garden*

April

ACORN BANK GARDEN	*narcissi, wild flowers, blossom*
ANGLESEY ABBEY	*hyacinth garden, trees, shrubs*
BADDESLEY CLINTON	*daffodils*
BELTON HOUSE	*daffodils and spring wild flowers*
BODNANT	*camellias, rhododendrons, magnolias*
CHIRK CASTLE	*daffodils, magnolias, rhododendrons*
CLIVEDEN	*bulbs and spring-flowering shrubs*
COLBY WOODLAND GARDEN	*rhododendrons*
COLETON FISHACRE	*spring bulbs, wild flowers, camellias, magnolias, tender shrubs*
COTEHELE	*magnolias and spring bulbs*
ERDDIG	*old daffodil cultivars, National Collection of ivies*
FENTON HOUSE	*spring border, blossom*
GLENDURGAN	*rhododendrons, camellias and spring bulbs*
HANBURY HALL	*daffodils*
HARDWICK HALL	*daffodils in orchard*
KILLERTON	*rhododendrons*
KNIGHTSHAYES GARDENS	*magnolias and spring bulbs*
LANHYDROCK	*magnolias and rhododendrons*
MOSELEY OLD HALL	*spring bulbs*

NOSTELL PRIORY	*rhododendrons*
NYMANS GARDEN	*rhododendrons, magnolias, camellias, rare shrubs and spring bulbs*
OSTERLEY PARK	*daffodils, bluebells, rhododendrons*
PENRHYN CASTLE	*spring wild flowers and daffodils*
PETWORTH HOUSE	*spring bulbs and wild flowers*
PLAS NEWYDD	*spring garden, rhododendron garden*
SALTRAM	*spring bulbs*
SHUGBOROUGH	*mass plantings of daffodils*
SPEKE HALL	*bluebells and rhododendrons*
TATTON PARK	*rhododendrons*
TRENGWAINTON	*tender rhododendrons, magnolias*
WADDESDON MANOR	*narcissi and other bulbs*
WAKEHURST PLACE GARDEN	*spring bedding and rhododendrons*
WESTBURY COURT GARDEN	*bulbs and blossom*
WEST WYCOMBE PARK	*narcissi, landscape*
WINKWORTH ARBORETUM	*bluebells and azaleas*

May

ARLINGTON COURT	*spring-flowering bulbs and shrubs*
ATTINGHAM PARK	*rhododendrons*
BODNANT	*rhododendrons, azaleas and laburnum arch*
BUCKLAND ABBEY	*camellias and rhododendrons*
CLAREMONT LANDSCAPE GARDEN	*camellia terrace*
CLUMBER PARK	*rhododendrons*
DUDMASTON	*rhododendrons and azaleas*
EMMETTS GARDEN	*rhododendrons, azaleas, magnolias and spring bulbs*
FLORENCE COURT	*spring flowers*
HANBURY HALL	*spring bulbs, cowslips and other wild flowers*
HARE HILL	*rhododendrons and spring-flowering shrubs*
KEDLESTON HALL	*rhododendrons and azaleas*
KINGSTON LACY	*rhododendrons and azaleas*
LEITH HILL	*rhododendrons, azaleas and magnolias*
MOMPESSON HOUSE	*magnolias*
PLAS NEWYDD	*rhododendron garden, spring shrubs*
PLAS-YN-RHIW	*camellias, rhododendrons, azaleas*

ROWALLANE GARDEN	*rhododendrons, azaleas, pieris and other spring shrubs*
RUFFORD OLD HALL	*rhododendrons and azaleas*
SCOTNEY CASTLE GARDEN	*rhododendrons, azaleas, kalmias*
SHUGBOROUGH	*rhododendrons*
STAGSHAW	*magnolias, rhododendrons and camellias*
TATTON PARK	*rhododendrons and camellias*
UPTON HOUSE	*spring flowers*
WALLINGTON	*spring-flowering shrubs*

June

ACORN BANK GARDEN	*herbs and roses, clematis*
BODNANT	*roses, water lilies, herbaceous borders*
CASTLE DROGO	*herbaceous borders*
CHARTWELL	*roses and late spring flowers*
CHIRK CASTLE	*roses and topiary*
THE COURTS	*roses and herbaceous borders*
CRAGSIDE	*rhododendrons*
EAST RIDDLESDEN	*philadelphus and lonicera*
GREYS COURT	*roses and pinks*
GUNBY HALL	*roses and herb garden*
HARDWICK HALL	*roses and herb garden*
LYME PARK	*massed formal bedding*
MOMPESSON HOUSE	*roses and mixed borders*
MOTTISFONT ABBEY GARDEN	*old shrub roses*
OVERBECKS	*tender herbaceous plants and shrubs*
PETWORTH HOUSE	*herbaceous borders*
SCOTNEY CASTLE GARDEN	*azaleas, kalmias and other spring shrubs, wild flowers*
SIZERGH CASTLE	*wild flowers, hardy ferns, roses, rock garden*
SNOWSHILL MANOR	*mixed borders*
UPTON HOUSE	*herbaceous plants*
THE VYNE	*roses, herbaceous border*
WESTBURY COURT GARDEN	*walled garden and parterre*

July

ANTONY	*roses, summer garden*
APPRENTICE HOUSE	*vegetable garden*
ARDRESS	*formal rose garden*
BADDESLEY CLINTON	*herbaceous borders*
BENINGBROUGH HALL	*formal garden, mixed borders, roses*
BLICKLING HALL	*formal roses, herbaceous borders*
CALKE ABBEY	*annual bedding and vegetables*
CANONS ASHBY	*roses and herbaceous borders*
CASTLE DROGO	*roses and herbaceous plants*
CASTLE WARD	*semi-tender plant colour*
CHARTWELL	*rose garden*
CLIVEDEN	*rose garden, water garden, herbaceous borders*
COLETON FISHACRE	*rill garden and formal terrace*
FARNBOROUGH HALL	*rose garden*
FELBRIGG HALL	*walled garden with herbaceous plants, roses and fruit trees*
FENTON HOUSE	*herbaceous borders, roses, vegetables*
HARDWICK HALL	*herb garden, herbaceous borders, roses*
HATCHLANDS	*summer rose garden*
HILL TOP	*colourful cottage garden*
KILLERTON	*herbaceous border, formal garden, tender plants*
LANHYDROCK	*formal parterre, roses, herbaceous borders*
LITTLE MORETON HALL	*flowers and vegetables*
LYTES CARY	*herbaceous borders*
MONTACUTE HOUSE	*mixed borders, roses and formal garden*
MOUNT STEWART	*Italian garden with herbaceous plants and roses, extensive formal and informal gardens with lake*
NYMANS GARDEN	*summer borders*
OVERBECKS	*colourful herbaceous borders*
PACKWOOD HOUSE	*herbaceous border, topiary*
PECKOVER HOUSE	*mixed borders, clematis and roses*
POLESDEN LACEY	*rose garden and herbaceous borders*
POWIS CASTLE	*container planting and herbaceous planting*

SHUGBOROUGH	*roses garden*
SPEKE HALL	*rose garden and herbaceous borders*
SPRINGHILL	*roses, herbaceous borders, herbs*
UPTON HOUSE	*herbaceous and mixed borders, water garden, vegetables*
THE VYNE	*herbaceous border*
WADDESDON MANOR	*terrace bedding*
WALLINGTON	*mixed borders, stream garden, conservatory*

August

ASCOTT	*formal bedding, mixed borders*
BIDDULPH GRANGE GARDEN	*dahlia walk*
CROFT CASTLE	*cyclamen bordering drive*
DUNHAM MASSEY	*courtyard climbers and borders, waterside planting, bedding, hydrangeas*
DUNSTER CASTLE	*mixed borders, shrubs, conservatory, citrus collection*
ERDDIG	*fruit trees, formal bedding, flower borders*
GUNBY HALL	*herbaceous plants*
HARDWICK HALL	*borders*
OVERBECKS	*mixed borders, many tender plants*
PENRHYN CASTLE	*eucryphias, fuchsias and tender plants*
POWIS CASTLE	*herbaceous and tender plants, container planting*
ROWALLANE GARDEN	*penstemon collection*
TATTON PARK	*formal parterre, mixed borders, roses*
TRELISSICK	*mixed borders, hydrangeas*

September and October

ANGLESEY ABBEY	*dahlias*
BIDDULPH GRANGE GARDEN	*dahlia walk*
BODNANT	*autumn colour*
ERDDIG	*fruit trees*
FELBRIGG HALL	*National Collection of colchicum, fruit trees*
HARDWICK HALL	*borders*
PECKOVER HOUSE	*fuchsias*

POWIS CASTLE	*herbaceous and tender plants, autumn border*
UPTON HOUSE	*aster collection, fruit trees*
WESTBURY COURT GARDEN	*fruit trees*

October

CLIVEDEN	*autumn colour*
CLUMBER PARK	*autumn colour*
FLORENCE COURT	*autumn colour*
KNIGHTSHAYES GARDENS	*autumn colour*
OSTERLEY PARK	*autumn colour*
PETWORTH HOUSE	*autumn colour*
PLAS NEWYDD	*autumn colour*
ROWALLANE GARDEN	*autumn colour*
SCOTNEY CASTLE GARDEN	*autumn colour*
SHEFFIELD PARK GARDEN	*autumn colour*
SHUGBOROUGH	*autumn colour*
STOURHEAD	*autumn colour*
TATTON PARK	*autumn colour*
WAKEHURST PLACE GARDEN	*autumn colour*
WALLINGTON	*autumn colour*
WINKWORTH ARBORETUM	*autumn colour*

National Trust Gardens by Category

Gardens & parks with early formal features

ASHDOWN HOUSE, *Oxfordshire*
BADDESLEY CLINTON, *Warwickshire*
BELTON HOUSE, *Lincolnshire*
BLICKLING HALL, *Norfolk*
CANONS ASHBY, *Northamptonshire*
CASTLE WARD, *Co. Down*
CHIRK CASTLE, *Clwyd*
CLEVEDON COURT, *Avon*
CLIVEDEN, *Buckinghamshire*
COTEHELE, *Cornwall*
DUNHAM MASSEY, *Cheshire*
DUNSTER CASTLE, *Somerset*
ERDDIG, *Clwyd*
GUNBY HALL, *Lincolnshire*
HAM HOUSE, *London*
HARDWICK HALL, *Derbyshire*
IGHTHAM MOTE, *Kent*
LITTLE MORETON HALL, *Cheshire*
LYTES CARY, *Somerset*
MONTACUTE HOUSE, *Somerset*
MOTTISFONT ABBEY GARDEN, *Hampshire*
NUNNINGTON HALL, *Yorkshire*
OXBURGH HALL, *Norfolk*
PACKWOOD HOUSE, *Warwickshire*
POWIS CASTLE, *Powys*
STUDLEY ROYAL, *Yorkshire*
TRERICE, *Cornwall*
UPTON HOUSE, *Warwickshire*
WALLINGTON, *Northumberland*
WESTBURY COURT GARDEN, *Gloucestershire*

Gardens & parks with pre-Victorian landscape features

ANTONY, *Cornwall*
ARLINGTON COURT, *Devon*
ATTINGHAM PARK, *Shropshire*
BELTON HOUSE, *Lincolnshire*
BENINGBROUGH HALL, *Yorkshire*
BERRINGTON HALL, *Hereford & Worcester*
BLICKLING HALL, *Norfolk*
CALKE ABBEY, *Derbyshire*
CANONS ASHBY, *Northamptonshire*
CASTLE WARD, *Co. Down*
CHARLECOTE PARK, *Warwickshire*
CHARTWELL, *Kent*
CHIRK CASTLE, *Clwyd*
CLANDON PARK, *Surrey*
CLAREMONT LANDSCAPE GARDEN, *Surrey*
CLIVEDEN, *Buckinghamshire*
CLUMBER PARK, *Nottinghamshire*
CROFT CASTLE, *Hereford & Worcester*
DUDMASTON, *Shropshire*
DUNSTER CASTLE, *Somerset*
DYRHAM PARK, *Avon*
ERDDIG, *Clwyd*
FARNBOROUGH HALL, *Warwickshire*
FELBRIGG HALL, *Norfolk*
FLORENCE COURT, *Co. Fermanagh*
GREYS COURT, *Oxfordshire*
GUNBY HALL, *Lincolnshire*
HANBURY HALL, *Hereford & Worcester*
HARDWICK HALL, *Derbyshire*
HATCHLANDS PARK, *Surrey*
HUGHENDEN MANOR, *Buckinghamshire*
ICKWORTH, *Suffolk*
KEDLESTON HALL, *Derbyshire*
KILLERTON, *Devon*
KINGSTON LACY, *Dorset*
KNIGHTSHAYES GARDENS, *Devon*
LACOCK ABBEY, *Wiltshire*
LANHYDROCK, *Cornwall*
LYME PARK, *Cheshire*
MELFORD HALL, *Suffolk*
MONTACUTE HOUSE, *Somerset*
MOUNT STEWART, *Co. Down*

ORMESBY HALL, *Cleveland*
OSTERLEY PARK, *London*
PACKWOOD HOUSE, *Warwickshire*
PETWORTH, *West Sussex*
POLESDEN LACEY, *Surrey*
POWIS CASTLE, *Powys*
RIEVAULX TERRACE, *Yorkshire*
SALTRAM, *Devon*
SCOTNEY CASTLE GARDEN, *Kent*
SHEFFIELD PARK GARDEN, *East Sussex*
SHUGBOROUGH, *Staffordshire*
SIZERGH CASTLE, *Cumbria*
STOURHEAD, *Wiltshire*
STUDLEY ROYAL, *Yorkshire*
TATTON PARK, *Cheshire*
TRELISSICK, *Cornwall*
UPTON HOUSE, *Warwickshire*
THE VYNE, *Hampshire*
WALLINGTON, *Northumberland*
WEST WYCOMBE PARK, *Buckinghamshire*
WIMPOLE HALL, *Cambridgeshire*

Gardens with Victorian & Edwardian features

ARLINGTON COURT, *Devon*
ASCOTT, *Buckinghamshire*
BELTON HOUSE, *Lincolnshire*
BENINGBROUGH HALL, *Yorkshire*
BIDDULPH GRANGE, *Staffordshire*
BLICKLING HALL, *Norfolk*
BODNANT, *Clwyd*
CALKE ABBEY, *Derbyshire*
CANONS ASHBY, *Northamptonshire*
CHARLECOTE PARK, *Warwickshire*
CHARTWELL, *Kent*
CLEVEDON COURT, *Avon*
CLUMBER PARK, *Nottinghamshire*
COTEHELE, *Cornwall*
CRAGSIDE, *Northumberland*
DUNHAM MASSEY, *Cheshire*
FLORENCE COURT, *Co. Fermanagh*
GAWTHORPE HALL, *Lancashire*
GLENDURGAN, *Cornwall*

HATCHLANDS PARK, *Surrey*
HILL TOP, *Cumbria*
HUGHENDEN MANOR, *Buckinghamshire*
ICKWORTH, *Suffolk*
KILLERTON, *Devon*
KINGSTON LACY, *Dorset*
KNIGHTSHAYES GARDENS, *Devon*
LACOCK ABBEY, *Wiltshire*
LANHYDROCK, *Cornwall*
LYME PARK, *Cheshire*
MONTACUTE HOUSE, *Somerset*
NYMANS GARDEN, *West Sussex*
ORMESBY HALL, *Cleveland*
OXBURGH HALL, *Norfolk*
PACKWOOD HOUSE, *Warwickshire*
PECKOVER HOUSE, *Cambridgeshire*
PENRHYN CASTLE, *Gwynedd*
POWIS CASTLE, *Powys*
RUFFORD OLD HALL, *Lancashire*
SALTRAM, *Devon*
SCOTNEY CASTLE GARDEN, *Kent*
SHEFFIELD PARK GARDEN, *East Sussex*
SHUGBOROUGH, *Staffordshire*
SPEKE HALL, *Merseyside*
STANDEN, *West Sussex*
TATTON PARK, *Cheshire*
UPTON HOUSE, *Warwickshire*
WADDESDON MANOR, *Buckinghamshire*
WAKEHURST PLACE GARDEN, *West Sussex*

Inter-war gardens

ACORN BANK GARDEN, *Cumbria*
ANGLESEY ABBEY, *Cambridgeshire*
BATEMAN'S, *East Sussex*
BENTHALL HALL, *Shropshire*
BODNANT, *Clwyd*
CASTLE DROGO, *Devon*
CHARTWELL, *Kent*
CLEVEDON COURT, *Avon*
COLETON FISHACRE, *Devon*
COMPTON CASTLE, *Devon*
THE COURTS GARDEN, *Wiltshire*

DUDMASTON, *Shropshire*
EMMETTS GARDEN, *Kent*
GLENDURGAN GARDEN, *Cornwall*
GREAT CHALFIELD MANOR, *Wiltshire*
GUNBY HALL, *Lincolnshire*
HIDCOTE MANOR GARDEN, *Gloucestershire*
MELFORD HALL, *Suffolk*
MOTTISFONT ABBEY GARDEN, *Hampshire*
MOUNT STEWART, *Co. Down*
NYMANS GARDEN, *West Sussex*
OVERBECKS, *Devon*
PLAS NEWYDD, *Gwynedd*
ROWALLANE GARDEN, *Co. Down*
SALTRAM, *Devon*
SISSINGHURST GARDEN, *Kent*
SIZERGH CASTLE, *Cumbria*
SNOWSHILL MANOR, *Gloucestershire*
TINTINHULL, *Somerset*
TRELISSICK, *Cornwall*
TRENGWAINTON, *Cornwall*
WIGHTWICK MANOR, *West Midlands*

Post-war gardens

ANGLESEY ABBEY, *Cambridgeshire*
CHIRK CASTLE, *Clwyd*
DUNSTER CASTLE, *Somerset*
EAST RIDDLESDEN HALL, *Yorkshire*
GREYS COURT, *Oxfordshire*
HARE HILL, *Cheshire*
KNIGHTSHAYES GARDENS, *Devon*
LAMB HOUSE, *East Sussex*
MOMPESSON HOUSE, *Wiltshire*
MOTTISFONT ABBEY GARDEN, *Hampshire*
PLAS NEWYDD, *Gwynedd*
SISSINGHURST GARDEN, *Kent*

Rose gardens & rose beds

ARDRESS, *Co. Armagh*
BATEMAN'S, *East Sussex* (planned and planted by Rudyard Kipling)
BODNANT, *Clwyd*
CASTLE DROGO, *Devon*

CHARTWELL, *Kent*
CHIRK CASTLE, *Clwyd*
CLIVEDEN, *Buckinghamshire* (designed by Geoffrey Jellicoe for Lord and Lady Astor)
COTEHELE, *Cornwall*
EMMETTS GARDEN, *Kent*
FARNBOROUGH HALL, *Warwickshire*
FENTON HOUSE, *London*
FLORENCE COURT, *Co. Fermanagh*
GAWTHORPE HALL, *Lancashire*
GREYS COURT, *Oxfordshire*
GUNBY HALL, *Lincolnshire*
HARDWICK HALL, *Derbyshire*
HIDCOTE MANOR GARDEN, *Gloucestershire*
HUGHENDEN MANOR, *Buckinghamshire*
KEDLESTON HALL, *Derbyshire*
LAMB HOUSE, *East Sussex*
LANHYDROCK, *Cornwall*
LYME PARK, *Cheshire*
MOTTISFONT ABBEY GARDEN, *Hampshire (National Collection of ancestral species and 19th-century cultivars)*
NYMANS GARDEN, *West Sussex* (old shrub roses)
PECKOVER HOUSE, *Cambridgeshire*
POLESDEN LACEY, *Surrey* (Edwardian rose garden laid out by Mrs Ronald Greville)
POWIS CASTLE, *Powys*
RUFFORD OLD HALL, *Lancashire*
SHUGBOROUGH, *Staffordshire* (Victorian-style rose garden created by the NT in 1966)
SISSINGHURST GARDEN, *Kent*
SPEKE HALL, *Merseyside*
TATTON PARK, *Cheshire*
UPTON HOUSE, *Warwickshire*
WIGHTWICK MANOR, *West Midlands*
WIMPOLE HALL, *Cambridgeshire*

Herb gardens & borders

ACORN BANK GARDEN, *Cumbria*
BATEMAN'S, *East Sussex*
BUCKLAND ABBEY, *Devon*

CASTLE DROGO, *Devon*
CLUMBER PARK, *Nottinghamshire*
EAST RIDDLESDEN HALL, *Yorkshire*
FELBRIGG HALL, *Norfolk*
GUNBY HALL, *Lincolnshire*
HARDWICK HALL, *Derbyshire*
LITTLE MORETON HALL, *Cheshire*
MELFORD HALL, *Suffolk*
MOSELEY OLD HALL, *Staffordshire*
ST MICHAEL'S MOUNT, *Cornwall*
SCOTNEY CASTLE GARDEN, *Kent*
SISSINGHURST GARDEN, *Kent*
SNOWSHILL MANOR, *Gloucestershire*
SPRINGHILL, *Co. Londonderry*
WESTBURY COURT GARDEN, *Gloucestershire*

Fruit & vegetables

ACORN BANK GARDEN, *Cumbria* (fruit trees)
ATTINGHAM PARK, *Shropshire* (orchard and nut grove)
BADDESLEY CLINTON, *Warwickshire* (some fruit trees, nut grove)
BARRINGTON COURT, *Somerset*
BATEMAN'S, *East Sussex* (fruit trees)
BERRINGTON HALL, *Hereford & Worcester* (historic apple orchard)
CALKE ABBEY, *Derbyshire*
CANONS ASHBY, *Northamptonshire*
CHARTWELL, *Kent* (fruit trees)
CLUMBER PARK, *Nottinghamshire* (plan to replant kitchen garden)
COTEHELE, *Cornwall* (fruit trees)
EAST RIDDLESDEN HALL, *Yorkshire*
ERDDIG, *Clwyd* (orchards)
FELBRIGG HALL, *Norfolk* (some vegetables)
GREYS COURT, *Oxfordshire* (some vegetables)
GUNBY HALL, *Lincolnshire*
HAM HOUSE, *Surrey* (trained wall fruits)
HANBURY HALL, *Hereford & Worcester*
HARDWICK HALL, *Derbyshire* (orchard)
HIDCOTE MANOR GARDEN, *Gloucestershire* (orchards)

HILL TOP, *Cumbria*
LAMB HOUSE, *East Sussex*
LITTLE MORETON HALL, *Cheshire*
MOSELEY OLD HALL, *Staffordshire*
NUNNINGTON HALL, *Yorkshire* (fruit)
PECKOVER HOUSE, *Cambridgeshire* (some fruit trees)
POWIS CASTLE, *Powys* (pyramid apples and espalier pears)
RUFFORD OLD HALL, *Lancashire*
TINTINHULL GARDEN, *Somerset* (vegetables)
TRENGWAINTON, *Cornwall*
TRERICE, *Cornwall* (fruit)
UPTON HOUSE, *Warwickshire* (kitchen garden)
WALLINGTON, *Northumberland* (apple trees and wall fruit)
WESTBURY COURT GARDEN, *Gloucestershire* (trained wall fruits and trees)
WORDSWORTH HOUSE, *Cumbria*

Rare trees & shrubs

ANGLESEY ABBEY, *Cambridgeshire*
ASCOTT, *Buckinghamshire*
BENTHALL HALL, *Shropshire*
BIDDULPH GRANGE, *Staffordshire*
BLICKLING HALL, *Norfolk*
BODNANT, *Clwyd*
CASTLE WARD, *Co. Down*
CLEVEDON COURT, *Avon*
COLETON FISHACRE, *Devon*
COTEHELE, *Cornwall*
THE COURTS GARDEN, *Wiltshire*
DUDMASTON, *Shropshire*
DUNHAM MASSEY, *Cheshire*
DUNSTER CASTLE, *Somerset*
DYRHAM PARK, *Avon*
EMMETTS GARDEN, *Kent*
GLENDURGAN, *Cornwall*
HARE HILL, *Cheshire*
HIDCOTE MANOR GARDEN, *Gloucestershire*
KILLERTON, *Devon*
KNIGHTSHAYES GARDENS, *Devon*

LANHYDROCK, *Cornwall*
MELFORD HALL, *Suffolk*
MOUNT STEWART, *Co. Down*
NYMANS GARDEN, *West Sussex*
OVERBECKS, *Devon*
PENRHYN CASTLE, *Gwynedd*
PLAS NEWYDD, *Gwynedd*
POWIS CASTLE, *Powys*
ROWALLANE GARDEN, *Co. Down*
ST MICHAEL'S MOUNT, *Cornwall*
SALTRAM, *Devon*
SCOTNEY CASTLE GARDEN, *Kent*
SHEFFIELD PARK GARDEN, *East Sussex*
SISSINGHURST GARDEN, *Kent*
SIZERGH CASTLE, *Cumbria*
STAGSHAW GARDEN, *Cumbria*
STOURHEAD, *Wiltshire*
TATTON PARK, *Cheshire*
TRELISSICK, *Cornwall*
TRENGWAINTON, *Cornwall*
UPTON HOUSE, *Warwickshire*
WAKEHURST PLACE GARDEN, *West Sussex*
WALLINGTON, *Northumberland*
WINKWORTH ARBORETUM, *Surrey*

Water gardens & waterside planting

BIDDULPH GRANGE, *Staffordshire*
BODNANT, *Clwyd*
CASTLE WARD, *Co. Down*
CLIVEDEN, *Buckinghamshire*
COLETON FISHACRE, *Devon*
COTEHELE, *Cornwall*
THE COURTS GARDEN, *Wiltshire*
DUNHAM MASSEY, *Cheshire*
DUNSTER CASTLE, *Somerset*
DYRHAM PARK, *Avon*
SIZERGH CASTLE, *Cumbria*
SPEKE HALL, *Merseyside*
STUDLEY ROYAL, *Yorkshire*
UPTON HOUSE, *Warwickshire*
WAKEHURST PLACE GARDEN, *West Sussex*
WESTBURY COURT GARDEN, *Gloucestershire*

Herbaceous & mixed borders

ACORN BANK GARDEN, *Cumbria*
ANGLESEY ABBEY, *Cambridgeshire*
ANTONY, *Cornwall*
ARDRESS HOUSE, *Co. Armagh*
ARLINGTON COURT, *Devon*
ASCOTT, *Buckinghamshire*
BADDESLEY CLINTON, *Warwickshire*
BATEMAN'S, *East Sussex*
BENINGBROUGH HALL, *Yorkshire*
BLICKLING HALL, *Norfolk*
BODNANT, *Clwyd*
CALKE ABBEY, *Derbyshire*
CANONS ASHBY, *Northamptonshire*
CASTLE DROGO, *Devon*
CASTLE WARD, *Co. Down*
CHARLECOTE PARK, *Warwickshire*
CHARTWELL, *Kent*
CHIRK CASTLE, *Clwyd*
CLANDON PARK, *Surrey*
CLEVEDON COURT, *Avon*
CLIVEDEN, *Buckinghamshire*
COLETON FISHACRE, *Devon*
COTEHELE, *Cornwall*
THE COURTS GARDEN, *Wiltshire*
DUNHAM MASSEY, *Cheshire*
DYRHAM PARK, *Avon*
FELBRIGG HALL, *Norfolk*
FENTON HOUSE, *London*
GREYS COURT, *Oxfordshire*
GUNBY HALL, *Lincolnshire*
HANBURY HALL, *Hereford & Worcester*
HARDWICK HALL, *Derbyshire*
HIDCOTE MANOR GARDEN, *Gloucestershire*
ICKWORTH, *Suffolk*
KILLERTON, *Devon*
KNIGHTSHAYES GARDENS, *Devon*
LANHYDROCK, *Cornwall*
LYTES CARY MANOR, *Somerset*
MELFORD HALL, *Suffolk*
MONTACUTE HOUSE, *Somerset*
MOTTISFONT ABBEY GARDEN, *Hampshire*
MOUNT STEWART, *Co. Down*

NYMANS GARDEN, *West Sussex*
OVERBECKS, *Devon*
OXBURGH HALL, *Norfolk*
PACKWOOD HOUSE, *Warwickshire*
PECKOVER HOUSE, *Cambridgeshire*
PETWORTH HOUSE, *West Sussex*
POLESDEN LACEY, *Surrey*
POWIS CASTLE, *Powys*
ROWALLANE GARDEN, *Co. Down*
RUFFORD OLD HALL, *Lancashire*
SALTRAM, *Devon*
SCOTNEY CASTLE GARDEN, *Kent*
SHUGBOROUGH, *Staffordshire*
SISSINGHURST GARDEN, *Kent*
SIZERGH CASTLE, *Cumbria*
SPEKE HALL, *Merseyside*
SPRINGHILL, *Co. Londonderry*
STANDEN, *West Sussex*
TATTON PARK, *Cheshire*
TINTINHULL, *Somerset*
TRELISSICK, *Cornwall*
THE VYNE, *Hampshire*
UPTON HOUSE, *Warwickshire*
WAKEHURST PLACE GARDEN, *West Sussex*
WALLINGTON, *Northumberland*
WIGHTWICK MANOR, *West Midlands*

Topiary

ASCOTT, *Buckinghamshire*
BODNANT, *Clwyd*
CHIRK CASTLE, *Clwyd*
CLIVEDEN, *Buckinghamshire*
KNIGHTSHAYES GARDENS, *Devon*
MELFORD HALL, *Suffolk*
NYMANS GARDEN, *West Sussex*
PACKWOOD HOUSE, *Warwickshire*
POWIS CASTLE, *Powys*
WIGHTWICK MANOR, *West Midlands*

Rock gardens

BENTHALL HALL, *Shropshire*
CHIRK CASTLE, *Clwyd*
CLEVEDON COURT, *Avon*
CRAGSIDE, *Northumberland*
DUDMASTON, *Shropshire*
HIDCOTE MANOR GARDEN, *Gloucestershire*
KILLERTON, *Devon*
KNIGHTSHAYES GARDENS, *Devon*
POWIS CASTLE, *Powys*
ROWALLANE GARDEN, *Co. Down*
SIZERGH CASTLE, *Cumbria*
WADDESDON MANOR, *Buckinghamshire*

Conservatories

ACORN BANK GARDEN, *Cumbria*
ARLINGTON COURT, *Devon*
BENINGBROUGH HALL, *Yorkshire*
CHARLECOTE PARK, *Warwickshire*
CLIVEDEN, *Buckinghamshire*
CLUMBER PARK, *Nottinghamshire*
THE COURTS GARDEN, *Wiltshire*
DUNSTER CASTLE, *Somerset*
FELBRIGG HALL, *Norfolk*
GUNBY HALL, *Lincolnshire*
ICKWORTH, *Suffolk*
KNIGHTSHAYES GARDENS, *Devon*
NOSTELL PRIORY, *Yorkshire*
OSTERLEY PARK, *London*
OVERBECKS, *Devon*
PECKOVER HOUSE, *Cambridgeshire*
STANDEN, *West Sussex*
TATTON PARK, *Cheshire*
WALLINGTON, *Northumberland*

Orangeries

BELTON HOUSE, *Lincolnshire*
BLICKLING HALL, *Norfolk*
CALKE ABBEY, *Derbyshire*
CHARLECOTE PARK, *Warwickshire*
CLIVEDEN, *Buckinghamshire*
DUNHAM MASSEY, *Cheshire*
DYRHAM PARK, *Avon*
FELBRIGG HALL, *Norfolk*

HAM HOUSE, *London*
HANBURY HALL, *Hereford & Worcester*
ICKWORTH, *Suffolk*
KEDLESTON HALL, *Derbyshire*
KNOLE, *Kent*
LYME PARK, *Cheshire*
MONTACUTE HOUSE, *Somerset*
PECKOVER HOUSE, *Cambridgeshire*
POWIS CASTLE, *Powys*
SALTRAM, *Devon*
TATTON PARK, *Cheshire*
THE VYNE, *Hampshire*

Grottoes

ANGLESEY ABBEY, *Cambridgeshire*
BELTON HOUSE, *Lincolnshire*
BLICKLING HALL, *Norfolk*
BODNANT, *Clwyd*
CLANDON PARK, *Surrey*
CLAREMONT LANDSCAPE GARDEN, *Surrey*
CLIVEDEN, *Buckinghamshire*
MONTACUTE HOUSE, *Somerset*
NYMANS GARDEN, *West Sussex*
POWIS CASTLE, *Powys*
SALTRAM, *Devon*
SHUGBOROUGH, *Staffordshire*
STOURHEAD, *Wiltshire*
STUDLEY ROYAL, *Yorkshire*
TATTON PARK, *Cheshire*

Woody Plant Catalogue

The systematic cataloguing of trees in NT gardens began in 1976, enabling the NT to clarify its policies for tree conservation. The objective of identifying, tagging and computer tagging all trees has been achieved in 22 of the NT's major gardens and arboreta.

The gardens and arboreta catalogued are:

BIDDULPH GRANGE, *Staffordshire*
BODNANT, *Clwyd*
COLETON FISHACRE, *Devon*
COTEHELE, *Cornwall*

CRAGSIDE, *Northumberland*
EMMETTS GARDEN, *Kent*
GLENDURGAN, *Cornwall*
KILLERTON, *Devon*
KNIGHTSHAYES GARDENS, *Devon*
LANHYDROCK, *Cornwall*
MOUNT STEWART, *Co. Down*
NYMANS GARDEN, *West Sussex*
PENRHYN CASTLE, *Gwynedd*
PLAS NEWYDD, *Gwynedd*
POWIS CASTLE, *Powys*
ROWALLANE GARDEN, *Co. Down*
SHEFFIELD PARK GARDEN, *East Sussex*
STOURHEAD, *Wiltshire*
TATTON PARK, *Cheshire*
TRELISSICK, *Cornwall*
TRENGWAINTON, *Cornwall*
WINKWORTH ARBORETUM, *Surrey*

Head gardeners are responsible for recording new plantings and the loss of trees and for renewing tags. The 25,000 records held at the Royal Botanic Gardens, Kew, are updated annually.

National Council for the Conservation of Plants and Gardens (NCCPG) National Collections in National Trust gardens

Adiantum	TATTON PARK, Cheshire
Anemone *nemerosa cvs*	CLIVEDEN, Buckinghamshire
Asplenium *scolopendrium*	SIZERGH CASTLE, Cumbria
Aster	UPTON HOUSE, Warwickshire
Buxus	ICKWORTH, Suffolk
Catalpa	CLIVEDEN, Buckinghamshire
Colchicum	FELBRIGG HALL, Norfolk
Convallaria	CLIVEDEN, Buckinghamshire
Crocosmia	LANHYDROCK, Cornwall
Cystopteris	SIZERGH CASTLE, Cumbria
Dryopteris	SIZERGH CASTLE, Cumbria
Embothrium	BODNANT, Gwynedd
Eucryphia	BODNANT, Gwynedd
Hedera	ERDDIG, Clwyd

Hemerocallis	ANTONY, Cornwall
Magnolia	BODNANT, Gwynedd
Osmunda	SIZERGH CASTLE, Cumbria
Paeonia *ssp & primary hybrids*	HIDCOTE MANOR GARDEN, Gloucestershire
Penstemon *large-flowered cvs*	ROWALLANE GARDEN, Co. Down
Platanus	MOTTISFONT ABBEY GARDEN, Hampshire
Rhododendron *forrestii agg*	BODNANT, Gwynedd
Rhododendron *Ghent azaleas*	SHEFFIELD PARK GARDEN, East Sussex
Sambucus	WALLINGTON, Northumberland
Scabiosa *caucasica*	HARDWICK HALL, Derbyshire
Sorbus *aria & micromeles*	WINKWORTH ARBORETUM, Surrey

New Gardens

The National Trust has opened three more gardens since this Handbook was first published in 1991.

Barrington Court Garden

nr Ilminster, Somerset TA19 0NQ
Tel: Ilminster (01460) 241938

SOIL & TERRAIN: sandy loam over heavy clay
ALTITUDE: 9m (30ft)
GARDENERS: three full-time; 2 trainees
SPECIAL FEATURES: walled kitchen garden

Varied and enchanting garden dating from early 1920s. Laid out in a series of three contrasting 'rooms' inspired by a design for the whole property prepared by Gertrude Jekyll. Separate colour themes identify the individual rooms. Oranges and reds in the Lily Garden; soft pinks and mauves in the Iris Garden around a central sundial; and geometric beds of white, cream and silver in the White Garden. The buss stalls originally used for rearing veal calves now provide a perfect planting site for fragrant roses and other climbers. Magnificent walled kitchen garden contains trained wall fruit and numerous varieties of vegetables which are used in the restaurant.

BEST TIMES TO VISIT: May and June for Iris Garden. July and August for White Garden. Spring onwards for kitchen garden
SEASON: April to end September
PUBLICATIONS: Pamphlet with garden plan. Leaflet with recent history of the garden
ROUTES: Paths throughout garden
PLANT SALES: Plants and vegetables for sale
FACILITIES: Restaurant, WC
FACILITIES FOR DISABLED VISITORS: Garden and restaurant accessible and ideal for wheelchairs. Motorised buggy available. Braille guide

LOCATION: In Barrington village, 5m NE of Ilminster, off A303, 6m S of Curry Rivel on A378 between Taunton and Langport [193:ST397182]
OTHER GARDENS IN AREA: Montacute House, Lytes Cary Manor, Tintinhull House Garden

Cragside Formal Garden

Rothbury, Morpeth, Northumberland NE65 7PX
Tel: Rothbury (01669) 21267

SOIL & TERRAIN: sandy alluvial soil
ALTITUDE: 152m (500ft)
GARDENERS: same as Cragside House

SPECIAL FEATURES: orchard house, clock tower, rose loggia, Dahlia Walk, ferneries, carpet bedding

The formal garden is laid out in three terraces. The top one contains the ferneries which were originally entirely glazed. The middle terrace, fronted by a lawn, is dominated by the orchard house, containing Armstrong's rotating pots, and will be restored to a working example of a fruit house. The lower terrace is in the Italianate style and bordered by a fine collection of hollies with the rose loggia as the centre-piece. The garden is bounded by 36 acres of undulating parkland planted with specimen sycamores and beech trees.

BEST TIMES TO VISIT: July to September
PUBLICATIONS: Same as Cragside House
ROUTES: Accessible from main grounds only. Dogs not allowed
FACILITIES FOR DISABLED VISITORS: No wheelchair access

Wordsworth House

Main Street, Cockermouth, Cumbria CA10 1SP
Tel: Cockermouth (01900) 824805

SOIL & TERRAIN: neutral soil. Level terrain
ALTITUDE: 50m (164ft)
GARDENERS: one part-time
SPECIAL FEATURES: walled garden

The garden at Wordsworth House is laid out in a manner which reflects the style of gardening typical of the period around Wordsworth's birth in 1770. Covering an area of ¾ acre the garden, which was referred to in 'The Prelude', is a blend of North Country cottage-style plants in a framework typical of a Georgian town garden. The terrace walk with its view over the River Derwent was a favourite playground of the young Wordsworth and his sister Dorothy.

BEST TIMES TO VISIT: Late spring/early summer
SEASON: April to end October
PUBLICATIONS: Souvenir guide to property
ROUTES: Free wandering
FACILITIES: Tea-room, WCs, shop
FACILITIES FOR DISABLED VISITORS: Wheelchair access possible for garden but not for house. Guide dogs admitted
LOCATION: Cockermouth town, Main Street
OTHER GARDENS IN AREA: Acorn Bank Garden, Dalemain (not NT)

National Trust Gardening Books

Gardening Tips from the National Trust

The expertise of National Trust provides tips on planting in spring, training climbers, lawn renovation, organic pest control and much more.

Published in association with the National Trust

DORLING KINDERSLEY

The Complete Book of Dried Flowers
MALCOLM HILLIER AND COLIN HINTON

The complete guide to the techniques of drying and arranging flowers, with advice on how to grow flowers for drying.

The Complete Book of Herbs LESLEY BREMNESS

A practical guide to the cultivation and uses of herbs.

Flowers MALCOLM HILLIER

An inspirational guide to choosing, arranging and displaying fresh flowers.

MICHAEL JOSEPH

An English Rose Garden: Gardening with Roses at Mottisfont Abbey GRAHAM STUART THOMAS

PAVILION

A National Trust Book of Gardening PENELOPE HOBHOUSE

A new edition of the practical guide to the ideas and techniques that have won widespread acclaim for the gardens of the Trust.

Some Flowers
VITA SACKVILLE-WEST *(with illustrations by Graham Rust)*

Originally published in 1937, the author selected 25 'painter's flowers' and wrote about them in her own unique style.

Period Gardens PATRICK TAYLOR

The story of the history and painstaking restoration of a dozen classic gardens rescued from decay.

PITKIN

Temples of Delight: Stowe Landscape Gardens
JOHN MARTIN ROBINSON

The supreme creation of Georgian England, the gardens at Stowe are being restored by the National Trust and this book describes their evolution and significance.

ALAN SUTTON

Nymans: The Story of a Sussex Garden SHIRLEY NICHOLSON

The story of the involvement of the Messel family in an important chapter of garden history.

VIKING

The National Trust Book of the English Garden
RICHARD BISGROVE

Using the resource of the gardens of the National Trust, the author charts the development of the English garden through the ages.

WEIDENFELD AND NICOLSON

Traditional English Gardens ARABELLA LENNOX-BOYD

The English style of these 28 gardens in the care of the National Trust displays an astonishing array of gardening ideas.

Sissinghurst: Portrait of a Garden JANE BROWN

One of England's most celebrated gardens is recorded here in all its moods and seasons.

National Trust for Scotland Gardens

In addition to the gardens featured in this book the National Trust for Scotland cares for many spectacular gardens over the border. National Trust members gain free entry to NTS properties. The main NTS gardens are listed below in their county groupings.

INVEREWE GARDEN, *Ross & Cromarty*
LOCHALSH WOODLAND GARDEN, *Ross & Cromarty*
BRODIE CASTLE GARDEN, *Moray*
PITMEDDEN GARDEN, *Aberdeenshire*
CASTLE FRASER GARDEN, *Aberdeenshire*
DRUM CASTLE GARDEN, *Aberdeenshire*
CRATHES CASTLE GARDEN, *Kincardineshire*
HADDO HOUSE GARDEN, *Aberdeenshire*
LEITH HALL GARDEN, *Aberdeenshire*
FYVIE CASTLE GARDEN, *Aberdeenshire*
BRANKLYN GARDEN, *Perthshire*
BRODICK CASTLE GARDEN, *Isle of Arran*
CULZEAN CASTLE GARDEN, *Ayrshire*
GREENBANK GARDEN, *Glasgow*
THE HILL HOUSE GARDEN, *Dunbartonshire*
THREAVE GARDEN, *Kirkcudbrightshire*
FALKLAND PALACE GARDEN, *Fife*
KELLIE CASTLE GARDEN, *Fife*
HILL OF TARVIT GARDEN, *Fife*
MALLENY GARDEN, *Midlothian*
INVERESK LODGE GARDEN, *East Lothian*
PRIORWOOD GARDEN, *Roxburghshire*
HOUSE OF DUN GARDEN, *Angus*
ARDUAINE GARDEN, *Argyll*

Further details about any of these gardens can be obtained from the National Trust for Scotland at 5 Charlotte Square, Edinburgh EH2 4DU (tel. 0131-226 5922).

Index of Gardens

Acorn Bank Garden 115–16
Anglesey Abbey 105
Antony 13
Apprentice House Garden 85
Ardress 129
Arlington Court 14
Ascott 76–7
Attingham Park 57

Baddesley Clinton 86
Barrington Court Garden 168–9
Bateman's 33
Belton House 106
Beningbrough Hall 120
Benthall Hall 58
Berrington Hall 59
Biddulph Grange Garden 87
Blickling Hall 107
Bodnant Garden 60
Buckland Abbey 14–15

Calke Abbey 88–9
Canons Ashby House 89
Castle Drogo 15–16
Castle Ward 130
Charlecote Park 90
Chartwell 34
Chirk Castle 61–2
Clandon Park 34–5
Claremont Landscape Garden 35–6
Clevedon Court 62
Cliveden 77–8
Clumber Park 91
Colby Woodland Garden 63
Coleton Fishacre Garden 16–17
Cotehele 17–18
The Courts 36–7
Cragside House 121–2
Cragside Formal Garden 169
Croft Castle 63–4

Dudmaston 64–5
Dunham Massey 92
Dunster Castle 18–19
Dyrham Park 65

East Riddlesden Hall 122
Emmetts Garden 37–8
Erddig 66

Farnborough Hall 93
Felbrigg Hall 108
Fenton House 78–9
Florence Court 131

Glendurgan 19–20
Greys Court 79–80
Gunby Hall 109

Ham House 38–9
Hanbury Hall 67
Hardwick Hall 94–5
Hare Hill Garden 95
Hatchlands Park 39–40
Hidcote Manor Garden 68
Hill Top 116
Hinton Ampner 40–1
Hughenden Manor 80

Ickworth 110

Ightham Mote 41

Kedleston Hall 96
Killerton 20
Kingston Lacy 21
Knightshayes Gardens 22

Lacock Abbey 42
Lamb House 42–3
Lanhydrock 23
Little Moreton Hall 96–7
Lyme Park 97–8
Lytes Cary Manor 24

Melford Hall 111
Mompesson House 43–4
Monk's House 44
Montacute House 25
Moseley Old Hall 98–9
Mottisfont Abbey Garden 45–6
Mount Stewart 132

Nostell Priory 123
Nunnington Hall 123–4
Nymans Garden 46

Ormesby Hall 124–5
Osterley Park 81
Overbecks 26
Oxburgh Hall 111–12

Packwood House 99–100
Peckover House 112–13
Penrhyn Castle 69
Petworth House 47
Plas Newydd 70
Plas-yn-Rhiw 71
Polesden Lacey 48
Powis Castle 72

Rievaulx Terrace and Temples 125–6
Rowallane Garden 133–4
Rufford Old Hall 117

St Michael's Mount 27
Saltram 27–8
Scotney Castle Garden 49
Sheffield Park Garden 50
Shugborough 100–1
Sissinghurst Garden 51–2
Sizergh Castle 118
Snowshill Manor 73
Speke Hall 119
Springhill 134
Standen 52
Stourhead 53
Stowe Landscape Gardens 82
Studley Royal 126–7

Tatton Park 101–2
Tintinhull House Garden 28–9
Trelissick 29–30
Trengwainton 30–1
Trerice 31–2

Upton House 102–3

The Vyne 54

Waddesdon Manor 83
Wakehurst Place Garden 55
Wallington 127–8
The Weir 74
Westbury Court Garden 75
West Wycombe Park 84
Wightwick Manor 103–4
Wimpole Hall 113–14
Winkworth Arboretum 56
Wordsworth House 170